STORMS OF PERFECTION
VOLUME II

STORMS OF PERFECTION

VOLUME II

ANDY ANDREWS

Distributed by:
INTERNET SERVICES CORPORATION
USA
BK406

Distributed to the trade by

DISTRIBUTION SERVICE

Books are available at quantity discounts to schools, civic organizations, corporations, and small businesses. For information please write to: Marketing Division, Lightning Crown Publishers, P.O. Box 17321, Nashville, TN 37217.

Published in Nashville, Tennessee
by Lightning Crown Publishers
P.O. Box 17321, Nashville, TN 37217.

The Bible verses used in this publication are from the New American Standard Version and the New King James Version. Used by permission.

Printed in the United States of America.

FIRST EDITION
First Printing: June 1994
Second Printing: July 1994
Library of Congress Catalog Card Number: 94-75820
ISBN 0-9620620-3-1

Editor: Robert D. Smith
Book Design: Barbara Payne
Cover Photos: Karla Dudley

LIGHTNING CROWN
PUBLISHERS

P.O. Box 17321 • Nashville, TN 37217
1-800-726-2639

What They're Saying...

*"It is almost impossible for me to express my enthusiasm for **Storms of Perfection**. This book will help anyone to achieve overwhelming success, simply by following the success secrets hidden within these pages."*
Orville Redenbacher
FOUNDER OF ORVILLE REDENBACHER'S GOURMET POPPING CORN

*"**Storms of Perfection** is a book from which to draw strength. A must read!"*
Rocky Bleier
FORMER NFL RUNNING BACK

*"James Allen wrote, 'Dream lofty dreams and as you dream, so shall you become!' **Storms of Perfection** embodies that sentiment to perfection!"*
Pete Babcock
VICE PRESIDENT & GENERAL MANAGER OF THE ATLANTA HAWKS

*"If you like reading other people's mail – **Storms of Perfection** is for you. This book is a motivator."*
Phyllis Diller
ENTERTAINER / COMEDIENNE

*"The ideas and principles of **Storms of Perfection** are inspiring, especially because they are expressed in the words of the people who live them."*
Tom Monaghan
FOUNDER OF DOMINO'S PIZZA, INC.

"Very inspirational stories for those trying to succeed in any field or life in general."
Coach Joe Paterno
HEAD FOOTBALL COACH – PENN STATE UNIVERSITY

"Inspiring stories to help every reader rise above problems. A valuable collection of fifty-two achievements perfect for every bookshelf."
Robin Leach
HOST, LIFESTYLES OF THE RICH AND FAMOUS

*"**Storms of Perfection** is a wonderful idea that should have been done many years ago. I love reading about the success of others, and this book will be an inspiration to many."*
Crystal Gayle
ENTERTAINER

TABLE OF CONTENTS

ACKNOWLEDGEMENTS

Thank you to my wife, Polly, and my manager, Robert D. Smith, who both played an important and critical part in the areas of encouragement, instruction, and inspiration.

Special thanks to Isabel Galindo, Alejandra Galindo, Sandie Dorff, Katrina Anderson, Carson Poindexter, Chad Poindexter and Lynsey McCorvey for their creative input in all phases of this production.

Special acknowledgement to Martha Luker Hales for her expertise and brilliant editing.

My sincere appreciation goes to Matt Baugher, Sally Geymuller, Cathy Gordon, Lois Hunter, Helen Hyatt, Alice Karron, Caren Kinder, Dana Kyle, Kathy Masamitsu, Lora McCarthy, Eric McClenaghan, Kelly McHugh, Joyce Milsap, Bob Novotny, Linda Perret, Ann Peters, Jackie Peters, Jan Ries, Alan Rohrbach, Cindy Siegfried, Jackie Steele, Sally Treece, Kevin Triplett, Michael A. Vander Werf, Emilie Webb, and Richard Woods for their invaluable assistance, advice, and help with the letter participants.

Grateful acknowledgement is expressed to Danita Allen, Jerry Allen, Lucy Andrews, Harry Brooks, Rick & Sue Carper, Jeff Davidson, Rocky Evans, Tim & Connie Foley, Kathy Fort, Robert Howard, Ellis & Doraine Lucas, Bubba & Sandy Pratt, Bart & Cherry Starr, and Dexter & Birdie Yager for their encouragement and belief in this project.

PREFACE

(EDITOR'S NOTE: This preface is reprinted from **Storms of Perfection I** in order to explain the concept of the title.)

I was seven years old, barely keeping pace as my father strode purposefully through the woods, the dry brush crackling under our feet. August was rarely pleasant in the deep South, but this year had been especially hot; especially dry.

Walking the densely forested stand of timber that day, young as I was, I was acutely aware of my father's mood. The month-long drought our area was experiencing had him worried. I watched in silence as he broke dry twigs from seemingly lifeless trees and examined the wilting, dull color of the new growth under them. We hiked through the dust of the parched creek bed, following it to the beaver pond where our family often came for picnics. The pond was nearly empty and the beaver lodge, usually a site of frantic activity, stood abandoned on dry land.

Without warning, the wind shifted. With the change in direction came a rapid increase in velocity and a perceptible drop in temperature. It became cool within a matter of seconds, as the wind, whistling above, threatened to send branches crashing down around us. Lightning and thunder worked the atmosphere almost simultaneously, creating explosions of light and sound that terrified me. My father, his arms wrapped around me tightly, was also afraid...and grateful.

He was grateful for this violent performance of nature and the hope of water that came with it. As the trees bent with the wind and the thunder covered my cries, my father sat down, pulled me into his lap and said, "Don't worry. You'll be all right. Something good is going to come out of this. Be still. Be patient."

As he comforted me, the rain came. Not with the gentle drops I had seen in the past, but in wild, silver sheets bursting all around us. It wound through the limbs and leaves, over rocks and deep into the tangled thickets leaving nothing untouched.

And then, as suddenly as it had begun – it was over. The thunder and lightning and wind and rain were gone, their energy exhausted. It was still again, but even at my young age, I noticed a difference. The forest wasn't just still...it was calm.

With his hand, my father wiped the drops of water from my face. Only my deep sobs betrayed the presence of tears, not raindrops, on my cheeks. Then he smiled, wrung out the front of his shirt, and motioned toward the pond. "It'll fill back up now," he said, "and those beavers will be able to spend the winter here like they'd planned."

We turned in time to see a doe and her fawn drinking from the already flowing creek. The frogs had started their own chorus as we headed for home. "Ahh," my father breathed deeply, "everything just smells clean, doesn't it?" And it did. The very air, which only a short time ago had been hot and dirty, now seemed almost sweet. "Let's sit down by this big oak, Son," he said quietly. "I have something to tell you."

I snuggled in beside him, and in very nearly a whisper, he began. "You know," he said, watching me from the corner of his eye, "you weren't the only one scared a little while ago. Those deer were afraid, too. The squirrels huddled together as close as they could get and what with all the crashes and booms, well, I'm pretty sure the rabbits were worried. But now, something important has happened. The very event that frightened everyone in the forest turned out to be exactly what they needed."

"Do you hear the birds?" I nodded. "Remember how quiet they were before the rain? Now they're hopping around, chirping, drinking from puddles, and feasting on the worms that come out only when the ground is wet. The fish in the pond have more oxygen to breathe and cooler water to swim in. The dust that was on all the plants has been washed away so they are much cleaner for the rabbits and deer to eat. Nobody likes dirty food."

"In fact, Son, all of us are better off now than we were an hour ago. Just because of the storm. What looked like the worst – turned out to be the best. It was a storm of perfection."

*   *   *

My dad has been gone for well over a decade, but I can remember that day in the woods as if it happened this morning. Writing this now, I couldn't begin to count the instances I've had reason to recall his words. There have been many storms in my life; and some were more terrifying than that day when when I was seven. I do try, however, to keep my father's lesson in my heart. And it is easy to hear him tell me, "Don't worry. You'll be all right. Something good is going to come out of this. Be still. Be patient. It's only a storm of perfection."

AUTHOR'S NOTE

When the first **Storms of Perfection** was released three years ago, I was unprepared for the reaction. It seemed to be a book for which many people were waiting. The concept was simple: a collection of letters from over fifty of the world's most successful men and women. In their correspondence, they told the stories of problems and rejections they overcame before becoming successful.

The stories and challenges they faced seemed to come from every possible angle – thus relating to a wide variety of people. Soon, mail began arriving literally from all over the world. Letters told how the book affected marriages, businesses, and lives in a positive way. "I'll never quit now!" seemed to be a common theme. There were even letters and messages from those who had been, but were no longer, contemplating suicide.

The real story of the first book, however, was its more than two years in the making. I was turned down by over 600 people before finally accumulating the 52 letters needed for publication. Then I couldn't get a publisher...or a distributor. My own agency (William Morris) refused to represent me on the book. I thought, "My gosh, I've written a book about rejection – now I'm getting taught a lesson about it!"

The outcome, of course, was that **Storms of Perfection** became one of the few books in American publishing history to sell over 100,000 books before it ever reached the book store. It has been translated into Spanish and is distributed in Mexico, Europe, Australia, and the United Kingdom.

The success of the book is not something for which I take a great deal of credit. I just put it together by hanging in there while being told by everyone that it would never work. This, by the way, was a lesson I learned from the people who took the time to share their stories.

And now, Volume II. Many people have asked if it were easier this time. The answer is a definite yes and no! Yes, in the fact that I knew the concept was worthwhile. The letters help those who are hurting and provide encouragement for us all. So to that end, I was aware that in time, I would be led to 52 achievers who were to be included.

The "no" refers to the question of participation. In this book, 458 requests were made. It is interesting to note that of the 52 letters received, 21 were from people who had turned me down for Volume I.

For the record, the totals for both books reached 1,072. Of those requests, 194 were women and 106 were African American. The letters were not sorted through or picked over. When 52 letters arrived, the book went to press.

Neither were the letters edited. The participating correspondents were promised an exact reprint – typos and all. Obviously, any platforms or opinions expressed in the letters are not necessarily my own. All the letters do, however, have merit as an example of what a person can accomplish by using life's challenges to learn and grow.

As you turn the pages, remember that the men and women who elected to bare a part of their painful pasts became famous or wealthy because of their actions...but they became great due to their attitudes toward the difficulties in their lives.

Andy Andrews
Gulf Shores, Alabama

Dedicated to the memory of
Joyce S. Andrews,
my mother,
my first encourager.

H. NORMAN SCHWARZKOPF
GENERAL, U.S. ARMY
RETIRED

…was the Commander of Allied Forces in Operation Desert Shield and Operation Desert Storm.

General Norman Schwarzkopf is quite possibly the most popular military figure our country has produced in this century. His strong and decisive leadership during the Gulf War helped bring an early end to that conflict. History will record the skill with which the General coordinated a war effort in a country deeply suspicious of foreigners. He was also able to maintain the secrecy so critical to the success of our troops – not an easy task during America's first internationally televised war!

General Schwarzkopf, you might also be interested to know, has a great sense of humor. On several occasions, I have enjoyed spending time with him and his son, Christian. The General laughs easily and is extremely quick witted. He is not only one of my heroes, he has become one of my favorite people. And Christian is a terrific young man – that in itself says a lot about his father.

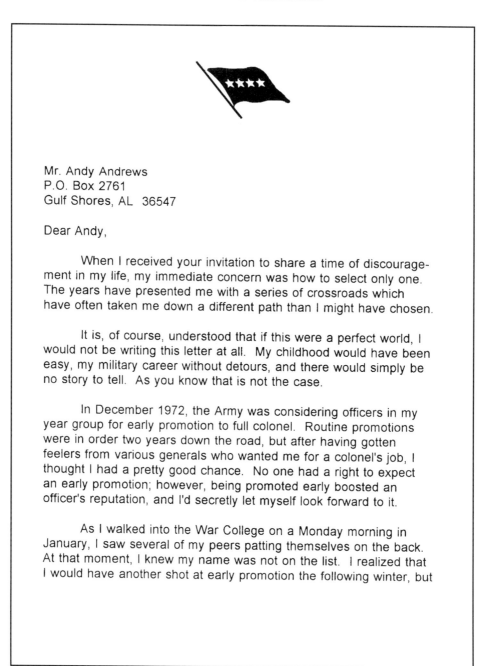

Mr. Andy Andrews
P.O. Box 2761
Gulf Shores, AL 36547

Dear Andy,

When I received your invitation to share a time of discouragement in my life, my immediate concern was how to select only one. The years have presented me with a series of crossroads which have often taken me down a different path than I might have chosen.

It is, of course, understood that if this were a perfect world, I would not be writing this letter at all. My childhood would have been easy, my military career without detours, and there would simply be no story to tell. As you know that is not the case.

In December 1972, the Army was considering officers in my year group for early promotion to full colonel. Routine promotions were in order two years down the road, but after having gotten feelers from various generals who wanted me for a colonel's job, I thought I had a pretty good chance. No one had a right to expect an early promotion; however, being promoted early boosted an officer's reputation, and I'd secretly let myself look forward to it.

As I walked into the War College on a Monday morning in January, I saw several of my peers patting themselves on the back. At that moment, I knew my name was not on the list. I realized that I would have another shot at early promotion the following winter, but this was the first time in my career when I was clearly no longer at the front of the pack. Friends offered condolences, which made me feel worse, as well as theories as to why I had been bypassed. I was disappointed, confused, and shaken.

The following November, I was nominated by the Army to serve as a military aide to Vice President Gerald Ford. I was honored and excited to be chosen out of all the lieutenant colonels in the Army. This was a prestigious job that would leave me with powerful connections in the event I decided to retire.

As the selection process went on, I got my hopes up. I was interviewed by the Vice President's assistant for national security affairs and even sat down with the Vice President himself. I thought we really hit it off.

In early January 1974, two events happened almost simultaneously. First, the Army released its list for early promotion to colonel and, to my shock, again I'd not been selected. Then, a few days later, I was called and told I had not been selected to work with Gerald Ford. In addition to the discouragement I felt, my frustration level was at an all time high.

At this point, I must tell you two of the most important lessons I learned from those and other challenges I have faced: (1) don't dwell on disappointment--deterimine to do your best anyway, and (2) we don't always know what's best.

Moving forward, I was soon commanding troops as a colonel in Alaska. This led to a troop command at Ft. Lewis, Washington, and promotion to brigadier general, followed by Pacific Command in Hawaii, and an assignment as assistant division commander of the 8th Mechanized Infantry--part of NATO's front-line defense in Germany.

After several other exciting assignments through the years, including command of the 24th Mechanized Infantry Division and participation in the Grenada student rescue operation, I took over Central Command headquartered in Tampa, Florida. My area of responsibility was the Middle East.

Looking back at my military career, I can see now that every struggle I endured pointed me toward my destiny in the Gulf War. The challenges we face in certain situations sometimes hold a purpose beyond our understanding at the time. We don't always know what's best. The tough times in my life often dealt with being put in positions not of my choosing, but the ultimate result is now a matter of history.

I am frequently asked if I miss the Army. I suppose the answer would have to be yes, but what I miss the most is the camaraderie of those who have suffered great adversity. This is the bond that links all old soldiers. Not surprisingly, it is also the bond that links successful people. Success without adversity is not only empty...it is not possible.

Sincerely,

H. Norman Schwarzkopf
General, U.S. Army, Retired

"Courage is resistance of fear,
mastery of fear –
not absence of fear."

Mark Twain

TOMMY SMOTHERS
ENTERTAINER

...is part of the longest lasting comedy team in history. The Smothers Brothers have a star on the Hollywood Walk of Fame. The Museum of Broadcasting in New York has produced a retrospective and seminar on their work.

Time has been an essential ingredient in the Smothers Brothers' success. They have been considered ahead of their time, masters of timing, and practitioners in timeless comedy. They recently marked their 35 year anniversary in show business, and now the Smothers Brothers are being saluted as time-honored legends.

I met Tom several years ago on the S/S Norway, where we were performing at opposite ends of the ship. I saw every show they did that week and was blown away. Since that time, I have done several concerts with Tom and Dick and even had the privilege of appearing on one of their CBS specials. As a comedian, I am often asked who I think is funny. The Smothers Brothers are always part of my answer.

I appreciate the time and effort that went into Tom's letter. The depth of feeling that he put into his words is obvious and I am certain that his purpose for this story will be realized. To re-live a period of embarrassment and fear is a tough thing to do, but Tom did it in such a way that brings hope to anyone in a similar situation.

Andy Andrews
P.O. Box 2761
Gulf Shores, AL   36542

Dear Andy,

This has been a struggle. I never realized how difficult it would be to open my heart and my past to you and your readers, but here goes:

My early years in school were tough. I was a slow reader, I couldn't spell or memorize, and numbers were a jumble. It took me three or four times longer to accomplish the same tasks as other kids - it was hopeless. I wasn't smart like everyone else. I was known as the "dumb one."

I wasn't aware at the time that I had a learning disability called dyslexia. Dyslexia can cause sequence problems in which letters and numbers are reversed. Memorizing can be difficult. Words like "was" would be interpreted as "saw." In any event, I didn't know that I had this handicap. School became a series of failures and my self-worth plummeted. I truly believed that I was stupid and worthless.

I became the fool. It was so easy to embrace the character, to become the under dog, the victim. Soon I was very good at it, in fact, I was brilliant. My visual and perceptive short circuits became my security blanket. I exceeded my own expectations by being funny and getting laughs. Being the "dumb one" was my way of coping with those painful grade school years.

It wasn't until I was thirty one years old and starring with my brother Dick on the Smothers Brothers Comedy Hour that I was formally diagnosed as having the learning disorder dyslexia. In any case, by then I had taken my "storm" and turned it into a gift. The sense of confusion, the halting delivery and fractured syntax, all the coping skills I had developed as a child to protect myself, had evolved into my comedic persona - my coat of many colors.

I have often wondered if I would have become a success without this "learning disability." And it also makes me wonder how many other challenges in life will turn out to be blessings in disguise.

Sincerely, your friend,

Tommy Smothers

KNAVE PRODUCTIONS INC.
8489 WEST THIRD STREET • SUITE 1020 • LOS ANGELES, CA 90048
(213) 651-5718 FAX: (213) 651-3503

7

CANDY LIGHTNER
AUTHOR/SPEAKER

...is the founder of Mothers Against Drunk Driving (MADD). She served as it's CEO, President, and Chairman of the Board until 1985.

In 1980, Candy Lightner was a successful real estate agent in Fair Oaks, California. On May 3 of that same year, her life was completely changed due to an accident caused by a drunk driver. Her initial grief and shock turned to anger when she realized the inequities of the criminal justice system in dealing with drunk drivers – particularly those with prior convictions.

Only four days after her daughter was killed, Candy began Mothers Against Drunk Driving. During her tenure, MADD grew to approximately 377 chapters with an annual budget of 12 million dollars.

Candy Lightner forged a national agreement on a divisive social issue which brought together both Republicans and Democrats. It resulted in the passage of over 500 bills at the state and national level including laws raising the drinking age to 21. Much of this legislation is credited with saving thousands of lives.

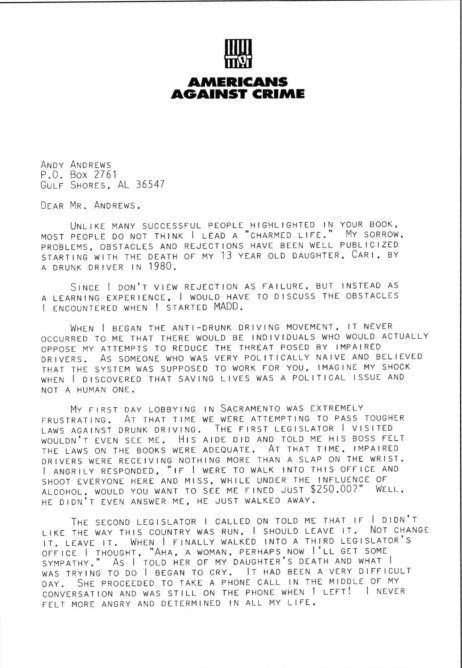

**AMERICANS
AGAINST CRIME**

Andy Andrews
P.O. Box 2761
Gulf Shores, AL 36547

Dear Mr. Andrews,

Unlike many successful people highlighted in your book, most people do not think I lead a "charmed life." My sorrow, problems, obstacles and rejections have been well publicized starting with the death of my 13 year old daughter, Cari, by a drunk driver in 1980.

Since I don't view rejection as failure, but instead as a learning experience, I would have to discuss the obstacles I encountered when I started MADD.

When I began the anti-drunk driving movement, it never occurred to me that there would be individuals who would actually oppose my attempts to reduce the threat posed by impaired drivers. As someone who was very politically naive and believed that the system was supposed to work for you, imagine my shock when I discovered that saving lives was a political issue and not a human one.

My first day lobbying in Sacramento was extremely frustrating. At that time we were attempting to pass tougher laws against drunk driving. The first legislator I visited wouldn't even see me. His aide did and told me his boss felt the laws on the books were adequate. At that time, impaired drivers were receiving nothing more than a slap on the wrist. I angrily responded, "If I were to walk into this office and shoot everyone here and miss, while under the influence of alcohol, would you want to see me fined just $250.00?" Well, he didn't even answer me, he just walked away.

The second legislator I called on told me that if I didn't like the way this country was run, I should leave it. Not change it, leave it. When I finally walked into a third legislator's office I thought, "Aha, a woman, perhaps now I'll get some sympathy." As I told her of my daughter's death and what I was trying to do I began to cry. It had been a very difficult day. She proceeded to take a phone call in the middle of my conversation and was still on the phone when I left! I never felt more angry and determined in all my life.

6060 Sunrise Vista East, Suite 3200, Citrus Heights, CA 95610 • (916) 967-1945

WELL OUR BILLS PASSED, LIVES HAVE BEEN SAVED AND ATTITUDES TOWARDS IMPAIRED DRIVING HAVE CHANGED. THOSE LEGISLATORS? THEY ARE STILL IN OFFICE - ONE EVEN WENT ON TO CONGRESS.

I RECENTLY HAVE STARTED A NEW ORGANIZATION, AMERICANS AGAINST CRIME, BECAUSE I KNOW WHAT A DIFFERENCE PASSION, DETERMINATION AND PERSEVERENCE CAN MAKE. SERIOUS AND VIOLENT CRIME HAS BECOME ALL TOO COMMONPLACE AND HAS MADE VICTIMS OF US ALL. I AM HOPING TO BREAK THROUGH THE APATHY ON THIS ISSUE AND HELP BRING ABOUT SOME MUCH NEEDED CHANGES IN OUR SYSTEM.

MADD TAUGHT ME MORE THAN JUST HOW TO LOBBY, SPEAK BEFORE AN AUDIENCE AND RUN AN INTERNATIONAL CORPORATION. IT TAUGHT ME THAT ONE PERSON CAN MAKE A DIFFERENCE.

SINCERELY,

Candy Lightner

CANDY LIGHTNER

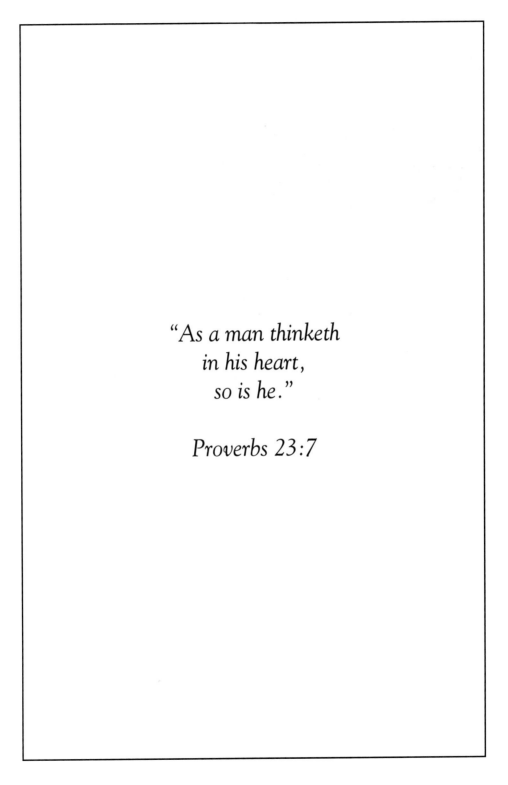

"As a man thinketh
in his heart,
so is he."

Proverbs 23:7

RICH DEVOS &
JAY VAN ANDEL
ENTREPRENEURS

…co-founded Amway Corporation in 1959. Now operating in more than 60 countries and territories, Amway is one of the world's largest network marketing companies.

Rich DeVos and Jay Van Andel are heroes to people all over the world. It is not only because of the work they have done for others; though their time committed to charity through the years has been enormous. Rich has served as the Finance Chairman for the Republican National Committee, as a member of the Presidential Commission on AIDS, and as Founding Chairman of the National Organization on Disability.

Jay has served as Chairman of the Board of the U.S. Chamber of Commerce. He is also the Director of the Gerald R. Ford Foundation and has been on the USO World Board of Governors.

Rich and his family now own the National Basketball Association's Orlando "Magic" and both men are annually listed among Forbes Magazine's wealthiest people, but the admiration for these two businessmen by people all over the world has come because of an opportunity they represent. The opportunity, of course, is Amway.

The Amway Corporation is privately held by the DeVos and Van Andel families. The company now employs over 11,000 people, but the opportunity to start one's own business is provided by Amway's commitment to free enterprise. Currently, over two million independent distributors are operating in over 60 countries and territories providing an example for their communities and freedom for their families.

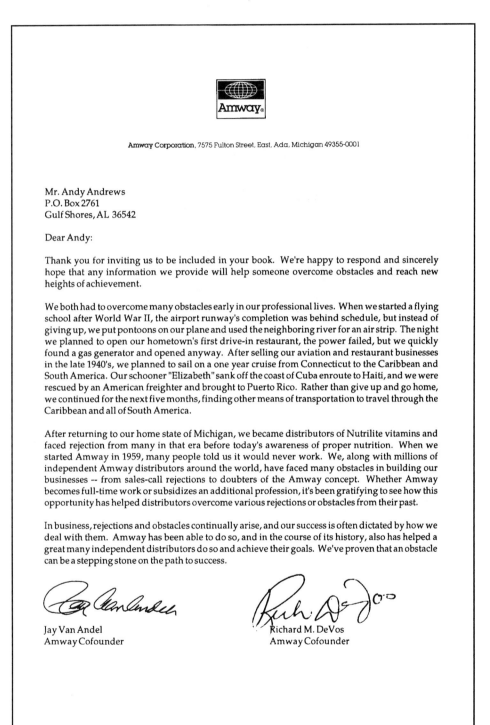

Amway Corporation, 7575 Fulton Street, East, Ada, Michigan 49355-0001

Mr. Andy Andrews
P.O. Box 2761
Gulf Shores, AL 36542

Dear Andy:

Thank you for inviting us to be included in your book. We're happy to respond and sincerely hope that any information we provide will help someone overcome obstacles and reach new heights of achievement.

We both had to overcome many obstacles early in our professional lives. When we started a flying school after World War II, the airport runway's completion was behind schedule, but instead of giving up, we put pontoons on our plane and used the neighboring river for an air strip. The night we planned to open our hometown's first drive-in restaurant, the power failed, but we quickly found a gas generator and opened anyway. After selling our aviation and restaurant businesses in the late 1940's, we planned to sail on a one year cruise from Connecticut to the Caribbean and South America. Our schooner "Elizabeth" sank off the coast of Cuba enroute to Haiti, and we were rescued by an American freighter and brought to Puerto Rico. Rather than give up and go home, we continued for the next five months, finding other means of transportation to travel through the Caribbean and all of South America.

After returning to our home state of Michigan, we became distributors of Nutrilite vitamins and faced rejection from many in that era before today's awareness of proper nutrition. When we started Amway in 1959, many people told us it would never work. We, along with millions of independent Amway distributors around the world, have faced many obstacles in building our businesses -- from sales-call rejections to doubters of the Amway concept. Whether Amway becomes full-time work or subsidizes an additional profession, it's been gratifying to see how this opportunity has helped distributors overcome various rejections or obstacles from their past.

In business, rejections and obstacles continually arise, and our success is often dictated by how we deal with them. Amway has been able to do so, and in the course of its history, also has helped a great many independent distributors do so and achieve their goals. We've proven that an obstacle can be a stepping stone on the path to success.

Jay Van Andel
Amway Cofounder

Richard M. DeVos
Amway Cofounder

JOHNNY RUTHERFORD
RACE CAR DRIVER

...has won the Indianapolis 500 three times. He has been in the Victory Circle at every major race track in the nation.

After reading Johnny Rutherford's letter, I am certain that no one would have blamed him had he never raced again. Certainly his wife, Betty, would have understood had he decided to retire after the almost fatal accident. But Johnny Rutherford is not a quitter. Within one year of that tragedy he went on to fulfill his dream...racing in the Indianapolis 500.

Johnny has since won the Indy 500 three times. He has had a total of 27 Indy car victories and ranks fifth on the all-time win list. In 1980, he won the National Driving Championship for Indy Car Competitors.

Johnny Rutherford has long been recognized as the Ambassador of Auto Racing. He represents many corporations in television and radio commercials and has worked as a racing analyst for ABC, CBS, NBC, and ESPN. He will tell you though, that his greatest accomplishments occurred because he continued to strive for success despite pain and discouragement.

Johnny Rutherford, Inc.

Mr. Andy Andrews
P. O. Box 2761
Gulf Shores, AL 36547

Dear Andy,
As you must know life certainly has its "ups" and "downs", and
anyone who has achieved success in his life is not exempt from
the "downs".

In 1966, the eighth year of my auto racing career, I felt I was
finally on my way to accomplishing my goals as a race driver.
The year before, I had won the United States Auto Club's
National Sprint Car Championship and had won my first Indy car
race in Atlanta, GA. I had signed a contract to drive in the
Indy 500 and the rest of the Indy car series for a premier team.
I would also be driving a new sprint car for the same owner that
I had driven for during the Championship run the year before.
How great life was!

The second sprint car race of the 1966 season was at Eldora
Speedway in Rossburg, Ohio on April 3rd. I'll never forget that
day! The promoter paid tribute to the 1966 Champion by
declaring "Johnny Rutherford Day" at the track. I had a new
car, but I was having difficulty in getting it "set up" to go as
comfortably quick as I wanted. In the feature race I was
struggling in the back of the pack when my team mate, Mario
Andretti, passed me for a position in my old car from the year
before. I was fighting to get into position to pass Mario when
the lights went out. Eldora was a dirt track notorious for the
rocks in the dirt. The spinning rear tires on Mario's car had
picked up a large rock and sent it in my direction. It hit my
goggles right between my eyes. I lost consciousness, and
immediately relaxed my foot off the throttle. Disaster follows if
deceleration occurs on a rutted dirt track. The car did hook
a rut, began a series of "flips" toward the guard rail, hit on top
of the guard rail, catapulted about twenty feet into the air
while going end for end very violently. It was so violent that
when the car hit the ground outside the race track and about
forty feet down an embankment in a creek bed, both of my arms
were broken. I also suffered a severe concussion, two broken
little fingers, and a "red out" (space term for breaking all of
the surface blood vessels in my head from pulling in excess of
10 negative G's).

To shorten the story, I was taken to a Dayton, Ohio hospital
where I was to remain for a month while having two major
surgeries on my arms. On the second day of my stay I asked my
wife, Betty, (who, incidently, is a registered nurse) to let me
see the newspaper with photos of "the crash". The headlines
read, "Rutherford Out For the Season". Well, I was incensed with
such nonsense. This was going to be my best year, and I would

15

be driving in the "Indy 500". I did--one year later!

That year was tough with nine major surgeries on my arms, but I never lost sight of the fact that I wanted to climb back into a race car and go fast. I had encouragement and help from many friends, but especially from my loving wife who nursed me back to health both mentally and physically. She's a very special lady! One only has to imagine what one can't do without the use of either arm for three or four months, to know how much help I needed and received.

It took some determination and perseverance, but I made it back to be blessed with a great many successes. Some of those successes were winning the Indianapolis 500 Mile Race three times, an Indy car National Championship, many victories at every major track in the country, and numerous other awards and honors. The Good Lord spared me that day, and maybe, just maybe, it really was "Johnny Rutherford Day". I know that I have appreciated my successes over the past thirty-four years so much more for having known the "down" time. Just never give up; never look back if you want to reach your goals. Profit can be gained from the "downs" to reach the "ups".

After reading your book, Storms of Perfection, I feel good knowing I am in such good company.

Thank You Sincerely,

Johnny Rutherford

"I believe in work,
hard work and
long hours of work.
Men do not break down
from overwork,
but from worry
and dissipation."

Charles Evans Hughes

GENE PERRET
COMEDY WRITER/ AUTHOR

…won three Emmy Awards for his work on THE CAROL BURNETT SHOW. He publishes a monthly newsletter for writers and humorists called ROUND TABLE.

Writing comedy is tough. Wait, let me rephrase that. Writing *good* comedy is tough. There are a lot of funny people in the world, but very few are consistent with the quality of material they produce. Gene Perret is a great comedy writer.

I was a great admirer of Gene's material before I ever knew who had written it. If you have laughed at Carol Burnett, Bill Cosby, or Bob Hope, the chances are good that Gene was the real genius behind their words.

Gene has authored nine books on the subject of comedy and humor and is also known as one of the most entertaining speakers on the banquet circuit. He is witty and warm, enchanting audiences with his hilarious anecdotes. Gene has been honored several times by Toastmasters International and was voted "Outstanding New Discovery in Humor" by the prestigious International Platform Association.

Gene Perret

Andy Andrews
P.O. Box 2761
Gulf Shores, AL 36547

Dear Andy,

As a third grader I tried out for our grade school basketball team. Generally, only the "big kids," the eighth graders, and occasionally an extraordinarily talented or tall seventh grader, made the squad. I had an in, however -- my older brother was coaching the team. If he cut me, I'd just tell Mom.

I did all right in all the drills -- running, dribbling, looking good in short pants -- until we came to the foul shooting exercise. The foul line in basketball is fifteen feet from the basket. I could only throw the ball about eight and a half feet. The harder I tried, the more laughs I got from the "big guys."

My brother, the coach -- my ace in the hole -- advised me to try to shoot the ball underhanded. Wise suggestion, I thought. Underhanded, I might reach the basket and that's all I needed because a family member was making the cuts.

I grabbed the ball with both hands and tossed it as hard as I could. It zoomed straight up into the air, hit the rafter, and ricocheted down onto my head. I cried, the "big guys" laughed, and my brother (giggling, too) comforted me.

I didn't make the team. I wasn't ready yet to play with the "big guys."

Years later I was writing comedy material for Phyllis Diller via the mail and over the phone. When I finally met her backstage at the Latin Casino in New Jersey, the first thing she said was, "Gene, you're my best writer." I was thrilled and complimented, but still cocky and arrogant. I said, "Phyllis, then how come I'm not in Hollywood?" She said, "Gene, you're not ready yet."

Phyllis was right. I learned when I did land a Hollywood writing job just how right she was. Others who debuted with me that year weren't ready and quickly disappeared.

Rejection is a reality in almost any undertaking that's worthwhile and it's always disappointing. However, rejection doesn't mean you can't or you won't; it simply means you're not yet ready. Like the puny little third grader, you haven't grown enough yet. You've got more work to do, more to learn.

I've learned from these experiences to be well prepared before making my move. I'd rather earn my success than have something handed to me that I'm not ready for. It pays bigger dividends in the long run.

Oh, incidentally, just to get even with my brother, I did tell my Mom what happened and she laughed, too.

Sincerely,

Gene Perret

"Work is as much a necessity
to man as eating and sleeping.
Even those who do nothing
that can be called work
still imagine that they are
doing something.
The world has not a man
who is an idler in his own eyes.

Humboldt

SANDI PATTI
ENTERTAINER

...is a five time Grammy award winner. She has recorded four gold and three platinum albums.

Many times in my life I have heard Sandi Patti referred to as "the most beloved voice in Gospel Music". She has one of those rare voices that can be described as an instrument unto itself.

Through her recordings, videos, and live concerts, Sandi Patti has touched the lives of millions of people. Over the years, her career has continued its meteoric climb. It has been highlighted by personal invitations to the White House, television appearances, and national acclaim as "America's Most Inspirational Vocalist".

Sandi's recording and performing style has garnered her an incredible thirty-two Dove awards over the last decade including ten consecutive years as Female Vocalist of the Year. It is hard to believe that a performer of this magnitude could have ever felt that she had nothing of significance to share.

Sandi Patti

Mr. Andy Andrews
P.O. Box 2761
Gulf Shores, AL 36547

Dear Andy:

What a great idea to have a book that presents honest struggles and not quick fixes! All of us, including those of us termed "celebrities," have had to overcome many obstacles to get where we are today and being honest about these situations is always the first step in building our confidence.

When I first got started professionally, I felt that I had nothing significant to share. Everyone around me, especially in the field of Gospel music, had these incredible stories of comeback and triumph. I was convinced that I was just a basic boring person, or so I thought. It's interesting how sometimes we create an atmosphere of perfection when, in reality, we are wrestling with hidden questions and insecurities.

In 1989, I began to experience real tests in my life. I could not have comprehended at the time that in the next few years, I would be praying for my two year old son as he was rushed into brain surgery; that I would literally watch our business office complex burn to the ground at the hands of an arsonist; that I would go through the painful task of identifying and finally dealing with a situation of sexual abuse as a child that has shaped my entire life; and that I would witness the death of my marriage, after thirteen years. In many ways, I began to question whether I had any remaining hope in my heart.

One of the most difficult things for me to deal with is that people think I've got it all together, and that I should be more vulnerable and let people in on some of these hard things in my life. I just never thought I could do that. However, here I am now, feeling like I'm totally exposed, but so grateful for the opportunity to take off any masks and just be me.

In reality, I probably found more hope than I ever had before. The struggles seemed to put things into perspective and help me realize that of all the things that grab for my attention on a daily basis, it is my faith, my friends and my family that hold the true importance. In many ways, I've made some good choices in my life and I've made some choices that were not so good. I'm proud of some of the things I've done and ashamed of some of the things I've done. But, in the midst of it all, God has been at work in my life. He continues to be at work in my life. That's enough for me.

I wish you peace,

Sandi Patti

SAM WYCHE
NFL HEAD COACH

...is the head coach of the Tampa Bay Buccaneers. He is also the co-owner of Sam Wyche Sports World in Greenville, South Carolina.

Sam Wyche is one of only nine current NFL head coaches to direct a team to the Super Bowl. He coached the Cincinnati Bengals to Super Bowl XXIII at the conclusion of the 1988 season. In eight seasons with the Bengals, he also claimed the 1990 AFC Central Division title.

Sam is known for his bold and innovative offensive strategies. In his over twenty years in the NFL, he has been associated with some of the game's most respected figures such as Paul Brown and Bill Walsh. To the knowledge acquired from them, he has added his own fresh style to create a scheme of offense that is unique and effective.

Sam's first season at Tampa Bay saw the Buc's offense improve nearly twenty percent in all important categories while moving up ten spots on the NFL list.

Earning a degree in Business Management from the University of South Carolina, Sam has put his education to good use in Greenville where he and a partner own a successful chain of eleven sporting goods stores known as Sam Wyche's Sports World.

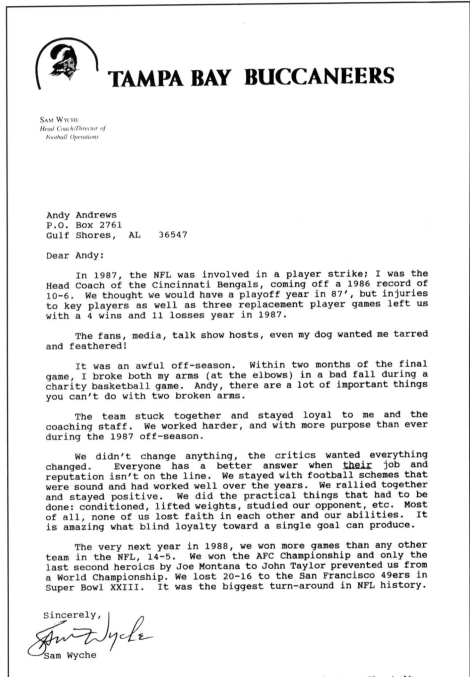

TAMPA BAY BUCCANEERS

SAM WYCHE
Head Coach/Director of
Football Operations

Andy Andrews
P.O. Box 2761
Gulf Shores, AL   36547

Dear Andy:

In 1987, the NFL was involved in a player strike; I was the Head Coach of the Cincinnati Bengals, coming off a 1986 record of 10-6. We thought we would have a playoff year in 87', but injuries to key players as well as three replacement player games left us with a 4 wins and 11 losses year in 1987.

The fans, media, talk show hosts, even my dog wanted me tarred and feathered!

It was an awful off-season. Within two months of the final game, I broke both my arms (at the elbows) in a bad fall during a charity basketball game. Andy, there are a lot of important things you can't do with two broken arms.

The team stuck together and stayed loyal to me and the coaching staff. We worked harder, and with more purpose than ever during the 1987 off-season.

We didn't change anything, the critics wanted everything changed. Everyone has a better answer when <u>their</u> job and reputation isn't on the line. We stayed with football schemes that were sound and had worked well over the years. We rallied together and stayed positive. We did the practical things that had to be done: conditioned, lifted weights, studied our opponent, etc. Most of all, none of us lost faith in each other and our abilities. It is amazing what blind loyalty toward a single goal can produce.

The very next year in 1988, we won more games than any other team in the NFL, 14-5. We won the AFC Championship and only the last second heroics by Joe Montana to John Taylor prevented us from a World Championship. We lost 20-16 to the San Francisco 49ers in Super Bowl XXIII. It was the biggest turn-around in NFL history.

Sincerely,

Sam Wyche
Sam Wyche

P.S. The fans, media, and my dog loved every minute. The talk show hosts found something else to complain about. And my broken arms were back to performing their usual chores.

25

RICKY SKAGGS
ENTERTAINER

...has been named the Country Music Association's Entertainer of the Year. He is a Grammy award winner and has numerous gold and platinum albums to his credit.

I am proud to say that Ricky is a friend of mine. Being an entertainer, I am often exposed to the offstage personalities of famous people. I hear how they really talk and what they really think. I see how they treat other people when the spotlight is off. On occasion, I have been disappointed—but never in Ricky.

Ricky Skaggs is a wonderful person. He truly cares about other people; their feelings, their perceptions, and their lives. With his wife, Sharon, Ricky is making more of a difference in the world today than ever before.

Ricky also has another side...one for which I am always on guard. Last year, when I was in the Caribbean, a friend and I were feeding fish in water up to our waists. A snorkler literally bumped into us and scared the fish away. The guy looked up, hair all over his mask, and said, "Gimmee some of that bread."

"We're out," I told him backing away.

He bumped into me again, splashing like a maniac. "Do you like cheese?" he said through his mask. "I do." Then he kicked hard at us with his flippers. "You know that Elvis guy?" he asked. We nodded (still backing away). "He's dead."

By this time, I was looking for a way—anyway—out. "Do you know who I am?" the stranger asked. We shook our heads, no. He took off his mask. It was Ricky. He has still not stopped laughing.

ENTERTAINMENT, INC.

Dear Andy,

I've never considered myself a very good writer, and I'm sure this letter will prove that. But I would like to share a few things from my heart.

In 1970, I left home to pursue a music career, I was sixteen. In 1972, I got married and put together my first band in 1974. That band broke up after two years, and my marriage broke up after seven years. I came to Nashville in 1980, got turned down by every record label in town except one...CBS. They signed me. I became one of those overnight success stories...yea right! I'd only been playing music for 22 years at that point. (I started in 1959 when I was 5-years old.) I was launched into super stardom literally within a year. I had a string of number-one singles, gold and platinum albums, at a time when the country music audience was about 20% of what it is today. In 1985, I was voted CMA Entertainer of the Year. Man, was everything going my way!

Then in 1986, my oldest son was shot in the mouth with a .38 caliber pistol by a drive by drugged-out truck driver. At that moment in my life, I felt the lowest I've ever felt. I really thought God had forgotten all the promises he had made me. But He proved His faithfulness again! My son recovered. He's 14-years old now, 6'1" tall and has his eyes set on being a University of Kentucky basketball player.

Then for some reason my record sales started dropping off, my concert ticket sales started to decline. The financial prosperity we were used to wasn't there anymore. So big changes had to be made. It seemed that everyone else was getting the big breaks...but not me. Everyone else was having the big record sales, the big crowds, the movie offers...not me. I felt as though I had gone from the guy critics credited with "puttin' the country back into country music in the 80's" to the guy forgotten. And again, I asked God "Where are you?"

P.O. Box 150871
Nashville, TN 37215
(615) 255-4563
FAX: (615) 248-6300

But again, I heard Him say, "I'll never leave or forsake you." So I got to thinkin', I believe this is a blessing from above, not a curse from below. The Lord was trying to teach me to trust Him...not my record label, or my booking agency, or my fans...but to trust in Him for everything.

So for the last seven years, I've been re-focusing my attention on family, friends, and establishing new relationships and accountability one to another.

I'm happier now than I've ever been. My wife, Sharon (who I married in '81) and I are having so much fun raising our children together. I love music more now that ever before, because now it has purpose, real meaning. I've seen how God has used my music to heal people (even physically), change their lives, their direction, give new hope, new vision, restore marriages, bring fathers and sons together again, and on...and on...and on.

I don't know what lies in store with my record label, my booking agency, or my career, but I know the changes I've gone through over the past seven years have all been for the best. I know that I won't let acceptance or rejection affect my music or my walk with God.

I know it takes storms in life to perfect us. I also know that I'm not perfected. But I'm glad to know that God loves me enough to stand by me when the storms come! He is faithful.

Ricky Skaggs

"*Folks who never do
any more than they get paid for,
never get paid
for any more than they do.*"

Elbert Hubbard

GENERAL CHUCK YEAGER (USAF Ret.)
TEST PILOT

...became the first man to fly faster than the speed of sound. He was also the first man to fly twice the speed of sound. He was awarded the Congressional Medal of Honor by President Ford and the Presidential Medal of Freedom by President Reagan.

Chuck Yeager has become a legend. After reading books and seeing movies about his life, it is difficult not to be awed by his accomplishments. General Yeager has flown 183 types of aircraft during his career. He has more than 11,000 hours of flight time, with over 10,300 of these in fighter jets. He is the only retired officer in America still allowed to fly military aircraft. He has recently flown the SR-71, the F-15, F-16, F-18, and the F-20 Tigershark.

When I first talked with the General about writing a letter for this book, he expressed doubts about having anything of significance to include. Needless to say, when I received and read the letter, I was extremely grateful for his participation.

Trying to put myself in his place, experiencing the challenge he describes, gives me a very real appreciation for what he has accomplished in his life. His words are a remarkable testimonial to why Chuck Yeager is one of the most highly decorated Generals of our time.

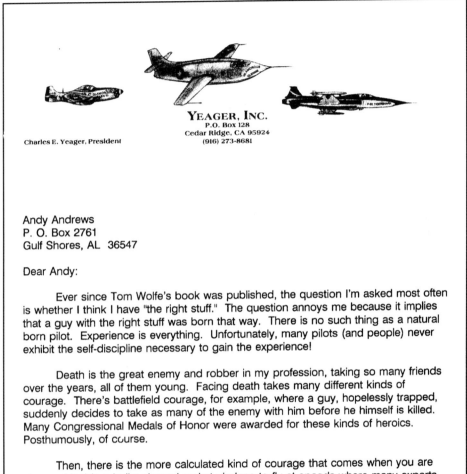

YEAGER, INC.
P.O. Box 128
Cedar Ridge, CA 95924
(916) 273-8681

Charles E. Yeager, President

Andy Andrews
P. O. Box 2761
Gulf Shores, AL 36547

Dear Andy:

Ever since Tom Wolfe's book was published, the question I'm asked most often is whether I think I have "the right stuff." The question annoys me because it implies that a guy with the right stuff was born that way. There is no such thing as a natural born pilot. Experience is everything. Unfortunately, many pilots (and people) never exhibit the self-discipline necessary to gain the experience!

Death is the great enemy and robber in my profession, taking so many friends over the years, all of them young. Facing death takes many different kinds of courage. There's battlefield courage, for example, where a guy, hopelessly trapped, suddenly decides to take as many of the enemy with him before he himself is killed. Many Congressional Medals of Honor were awarded for these kinds of heroics. Posthumously, of course.

Then, there is the more calculated kind of courage that comes when you are strapped inside a bullet-shaped rocket airplane to fly at speeds where many experts think the ship will disintegrate. At the time, I wouldn't have bet on my chances for winning the Medal of Honor, but the nice part about receiving it for me was that I received it standing up!

One of the secrets of my success has always been facing problems head on. An early chance to demonstrate that ability came during World War II, when I faced on of the toughest challenges of my life.

I had been shot down over Nazi Germany on March 5, 1944. After eluding capture for several days, I finally made contact with members of the French underground. For awhile, I lived in haylofts and sheds until one day I was taken to a group of heavily armed men. They were wearing black berets and bandoliers of rifle cartridges strapped across their chests. I didn't have to be told who these guys were. They were the Maquis, the French resistance fighters who lived and hid in the mountain forests by day and blew up trains and bridges by night.

Page 2

After staying with the Maquis for a time, they led me to a rendezvous at the base of the Pyrenees with several other fliers who had also managed to elude capture. We were told that we would have to cross the mountains alone to reach Spain. "Take the southern route," they said. "No fires, no talking. This place is patrolled." It was March twenty-third.

My companion was a lieutenant, a navigator on a B-24 shot down over France. The Pyrenees made the hills back in West Virginia look like straighaways! The highest peaks were eleven thousand feet but we figured we wouldn't get higher than six or seven thousand. The trouble was that we were up to our knees in wet, heavy snow.

At first we would rest every hour, then every half-hour, then every fifteen minutes. We slept when we could, using outcroppings in the rock to protect us from the constant, freezing wind. Finally, we found an abandoned lumberman's cabin and collapsed on the floor.

While we slept, a German patrol passed by the cabin. They asked no questions. They unslung their rifles and began firing through the front door. The first bullets whined above my head and thudded into the wall. I leapt through the rear window, my friend right behind me. Hearing him scream, I grabbed hold of him and yanked him with me as I jumped on a snow covered log slide. Spinning around in a cloud of snow, it seemed two miles to the end of that flume. We splashed down straight into a creek.

Fortunately, the water was deep. My partner was gray. He had been shot in the knee and was bleeding to death. I tore away his pant leg and couldn't believe it. His lower leg was attached to his upper leg by only a tendon. Using my penknife, I cut the tendon and used the extra shirt in my knapsack to tie around the stump.

He was unconscious, but still breathing and we were pretty well hidden from the Germans up above. I decided to wait until nightfall and somehow drag both of us back up that mountain and get us into Spain. I stopped often to see if my friend was still alive. Every muscle in my body hammered me. I wanted to just leg go of the guy and drop in my tracks -- either to sleep or die. I decided not to stop and rest. I didn't trust myself not to fall asleep and let go.

On a ridge, I walked to the edge and looked down a long sloping draw. Off in the distance, I saw the thin line of a road that I figured must be Spain. I hauled my partner to the edge, checked once more to see if he was breathing, and shoved him over the side. I watched him slide down until he was barely a dot in the snow and then slid after him.

Page 3

Figuring I had done all I could for him, I left him on the road where he could be found. I hiked another twenty miles to the nearest village, where after a brief run in with the local police, I slept for two days. The American consul woke me up. My friend, I was told, had been found and was fine. It was March 30, 1944.

Andy, this was not an easy time in my life, but one that certainly had value. I suppose it taught me a lesson of perseverance that I never forgot. Years later, as I became the first man to fly faster than the speed of sound, I remembered how I beat the first mountains in my life. I never quit...even when the evidence indicated that I should!

Sincerely,

Charles E. Yeager
Brig. Gen., USAF, Ret.

CEY/cs

LORIANNE CROOK
TELEVISION PERSONALITY

...is the co-host of "Music City Tonight" on TNN. She produces and appears on over 300 hours of television programming every year.

Lorianne is one of the nicest people I know. She is also one of the most talented. And the smartest.

Nice? Ask anyone in the entertainment industry, ask her husband Jim, ask her neighbors! Lorianne has a top-rated show on The Nashville Network due in large part to the feeling she generates with viewers. They love her and they know that she loves them. She is nice.

Talented? She is a producer, writer, and performer. Besides "Music City Tonight" which she co-hosts five nights a week with Charlie Chase, Lorianne produces and appears in specials for radio and television that are broadcast around the world.

Smart? Lorianne is a magna cum laude graduate of Vanderbilt University with a double major...Russian and Chinese. Need I say more?

I will. "The Cable Guide" has named her one of the "Ten Most Beautiful Women on Cable Television". They are right. By the way, I think Lorianne is terrific. Can you tell?

Andy Andrews
P.O. Box 2761
Gulf Shores, AL   36547

Dear Andy:

I enjoyed your first book immensely and am thrilled you
asked me to contribute to this one.

Let me start off by saying that things have gone unbelievably
well for me. I am only 36 years old and have already achieved
success way beyond my original goals.

Twelve years ago my intent was to dabble a bit in television
to see if I would be good enough to be a local news reporter
in my favorite city, Nashville, Tennessee. Since I majored
in foreign languages in college, I even thought I might be
lucky enough to someday become one of the many foreign
correspondents that cover world news.

Through a long series of life's twists and turns, I ended
up in the entertainment end of television. Today I am
elated to be the host, along with Charlie Chase, of the
prime time flagship show of The Nashville Network, MUSIC
CITY TONIGHT. An incredible 65 million homes are wired
into our show. Because of this position, I meet and work
with the most talented people in the world...singing stars
like Garth Brooks, Tony Bennett, and Reba McEntire...movie
stars like Kirk Douglas and Sylvester Stallone...and those
who are so famous on TV like Peter Jennings and Delta Burke.

What makes my career even more interesting and fulfilling is
that my husband and I own and operate the production company
that produces a large percentage of the top programs on TNN.
It's wonderful because I feel I have earned the trust and
respect of some very important people who allow me to present
their talent and pieces of their lives to the public.

"Earned" is the key word here. People often tell me how
lucky I am to have landed such a fun job. I'm sure luck
played some sort of role, but for 12 years I have truly
worked overtime and in overdrive to be good at writing,
producing, and hosting television shows. It has been

A Production of Jim Owens & Associates
1525 McGavock Street • Nashville, Tennessee 37203-3131
615/256-7700 • Fax 615/256-7779

challenging to get so far so fast, but it hasn't been the hard part.

The hard part has been realizing that not everyone is happy for you when you succeed. Once I got into the "big leagues" as they call it, it became apparent that other individuals and even other companies were jealous of our accomplishments. In both subtle and overt ways, I have seen others ignore the rules of friendly competition and try to damage us. We don't work that way, and it was amazing to realize that others do.

I used to feel very hurt a lot of the time knowing that others were "out to get us". But this has turned out to be one of the greatest ongoing lessons in my life...and it is a positive one. It has taught me in a very clear way that you can't allow people and events to ruin even a minute of your day, much less your life. In the same way, you can't depend upon others to make you happy.

No matter what is happening around you, be it good or bad, anything you need, you can pull from inside yourself. Why do you think that so many rich and famous people who seem to have it made appear to be so unhappy? They depend upon those "outside" things like wealth and fame to create their happiness. When you finally come to terms with the fact that you must be your own best counsel and your own best friend, you will find much more freedom and peace. Your relationships with others become more meaningful, yet they don't control you.

Let me add that there are many things that test this belief in myself on a daily basis!! There are times when it takes all you have to master your self control...but at least I don't live in fear of the next blow that life is going to deal me. I can go along happily knowing that I WILL be able to handle whatever comes my way.

I have my wonderful husband, Jim Owens, to thank for being a living example of this philosophy of life. Thanks Jim, I love you!

I love you too, Andy!

Lorianne Crook

Lorianne Crook

"Dost thou love life?
Then do not squander time,
for that is the stuff
life is made of."

Ben Franklin

DR. KEN BLANCHARD
AUTHOR/SPEAKER

...is chairman of Blanchard Training and Development, Inc. His books have been translated into twenty languages and have sold more than seven million copies.

Over the years, I have read a large number of "self help" books. Ken Blanchard's publications concerning business and people management have always impressed me as being easily understood. He gets his point across—and most importantly, I have always been able to apply the information.

His impact has been far reaching. His One Minute Manager Library, which includes THE ONE MINUTE MANAGER (1982), PUTTING THE ONE MINUTE MANAGER TO WORK (1984), LEADERSHIP AND THE ONE MINUTE MANAGER (1985), THE ONE MINUTE MANAGER GETS FIT (1986), and THE ONE MINUTE MANAGER MEETS THE MONKEY (1989) have sold millions.

A gregarious, sought after speaker and business consultant, he is universally characterized by friends and colleagues as one of the most powerful, insightful, and compassionate men in business today.

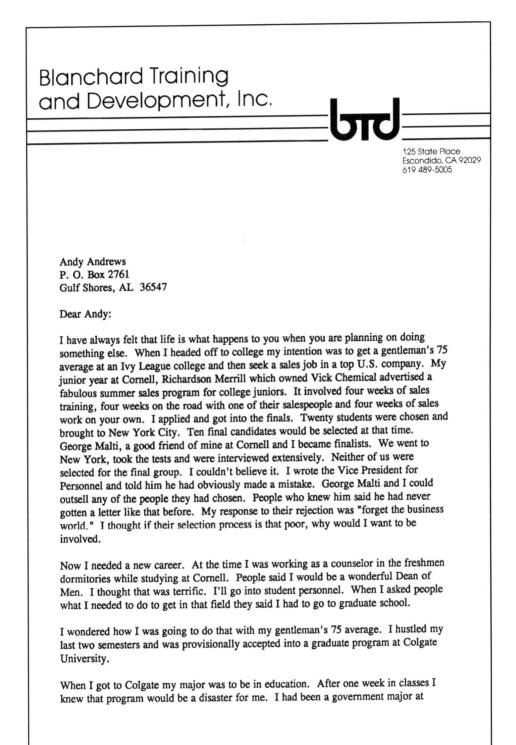

Blanchard Training and Development, Inc.

btd

125 State Place
Escondido, CA 92029
619 489-5005

Andy Andrews
P. O. Box 2761
Gulf Shores, AL 36547

Dear Andy:

I have always felt that life is what happens to you when you are planning on doing something else. When I headed off to college my intention was to get a gentleman's 75 average at an Ivy League college and then seek a sales job in a top U.S. company. My junior year at Cornell, Richardson Merrill which owned Vick Chemical advertised a fabulous summer sales program for college juniors. It involved four weeks of sales training, four weeks on the road with one of their salespeople and four weeks of sales work on your own. I applied and got into the finals. Twenty students were chosen and brought to New York City. Ten final candidates would be selected at that time. George Malti, a good friend of mine at Cornell and I became finalists. We went to New York, took the tests and were interviewed extensively. Neither of us were selected for the final group. I couldn't believe it. I wrote the Vice President for Personnel and told him he had obviously made a mistake. George Malti and I could outsell any of the people they had chosen. People who knew him said he had never gotten a letter like that before. My response to their rejection was "forget the business world." I thought if their selection process is that poor, why would I want to be involved.

Now I needed a new career. At the time I was working as a counselor in the freshmen dormitories while studying at Cornell. People said I would be a wonderful Dean of Men. I thought that was terrific. I'll go into student personnel. When I asked people what I needed to do to get in that field they said I had to go to graduate school.

I wondered how I was going to do that with my gentleman's 75 average. I hustled my last two semesters and was provisionally accepted into a graduate program at Colgate University.

When I got to Colgate my major was to be in education. After one week in classes I knew that program would be a disaster for me. I had been a government major at

Cornell where classes were lively and provocative. The education courses looked like real "snoozers."

One evening I found myself sitting at the bar at the Colgate Inn feeling sorry for myself and the unmotivating program I felt I was in. It was at that time I met Warren Ramshaw who had just joined the faculty at Colgate. He had just arrived on campus from the University of Illinois. His wife was still packing so he was staying at the Colgate Inn. Warren was in sociology. When I told him my dilemma he said, "Why don't you come and study with me.?"

"What a great idea. I'll major in sociology." Warren Ramshaw changed my whole career as I got excited about applying the social and behavioral sciences to organizational problems. As a result I got a Master's degree in sociology.

Now I was ready to be a Dean of Men. "What did I have to do now?" I thought. People said you had better get a doctor's degree. I said, "Doctor's degree. You've got to be kidding." I remember as an undergraduate watching the doctoral degree candidates walking across the stage. I had thought those people must be so smart. In reality what I learned is that graduate education is more endurance than intelligence. So I applied to Cornell for a graduate degree in educational leadership and was provisionally accepted again. My great undergraduate record and lousy test scores kept on coming back to haunt me. My chairman, Don McCarty told me the great advantage I had at Cornell was I could take a lot of courses outside the School of Education. I wandered all over campus in every behavioral science course I could get. When it came to graduation I was now ready to be a Dean of Students.

I went to Washington to the big national meeting of student personnel administrators. I had some wonderful job interviews with folks from Dartmouth, Wesleyan, Colorado State and several other institutions. All the jobs I wanted to interview for involved working closely with the faculty. My feeling was that student personnel administration was usually on the bottom floor of the administration building and that's about where it fit in the hierarchy. I thought the key to being effective in this field was to work closely with the faculty and be an expert on student environment. All of my interviewers said they were going to invite me to their campus. No one did.

I finally called one of the interviewers whom I had gotten to know quite well. I asked him why I hadn't been asked to campus. He said he felt bad. He had thought of calling me because I had two awful recommendations in my placement file. I asked from whom? He said the Dean of Students and the Associate Dean of Students. I couldn't believe it. I always thought I had a good relationship with both of them. The Dean of Students said in his recommendation, "Ken Blanchard is a wonderful guy. He's terrific in the dormitories but don't let him near the faculty. He has no academic interest." I took a course from this dean. We called it "Sleeping with Stan." It was an awful course and here he was attacking my academic interest. The Associate Dean of Students said, "Ken Blanchard is a wonderful guy; not particularly bright but great in

2

the dormitory area." As a result of those two letters I was "dead" in the student personnel market for that year. What was my reaction? "Forget student personnel. If they have people like that I don't want any part of it."

Now I was off career planning again. I chatted with Joe DiStefano who had been at Harvard Business School. He was getting a doctorate in social psychology. I explained my situation and he suggested I write to Vern Alden, president of Ohio University in Athens, Ohio. He had been at Harvard and was trying to make Ohio University the Harvard of the midwest. I wrote to Alden and he sent my letter off to Harry Evarts, dean of the College of Business. Harry called me and said, "Blanchard, you have a crazy background but we have a bunch of crazy people out here. I'd like you to come out and talk with me." Harry was looking for an administrative assistant to help him create a curriculum in administration. He felt that having separate programs in business administration, hospital administration, educational administration, public administration and the like was ridiculous. He felt there was more commonality between running organizations than differences. As a result, I headed off to Ohio University as a college administrator.

When I got to Athens, Ohio Harry said "I want you to teach at least one course. I like all my deans to teach." I had never thought about teaching since my faculty at Cornell had always told me my writing wasn't academic enough. (I later learned that you could understand it.) I felt if I couldn't write how would I survive as a faculty member. At any rate, Harry put me in a course in the management department and my life came alive as I got in front of students. That became my passion to be a "loving teacher of simple truths." This is a long way to tell you that any rejections I have gotten in life I have assumed were someone else's problem. I have immediately looked for another opportunity and moved forward without lowered self esteem. If you aren't your own best friend, who will be.

Hope these comments help. Feel free to edit, change, drop any part of it. Good on you.

Regards,

Ken Blanchard

Kenneth H. Blanchard

/et

DR. DENNIS KIMBRO
AUTHOR

...is known internationally as a best-selling author and speaker on the subject of African-Americans and their secrets of success.

Since 1985, Dr. Dennis Kimbro has combed the country interviewing many of Black America's most notable achievers. Dr. Kimbro is a native of New Jersey who has lived in Atlanta for the past ten years. He received his doctorate from Northwestern University where he studied wealth and poverty among underdeveloped countries.

Dr. Kimbro's honors include various awards bestowed by the business community such as "Who's Who in Black America" and the Dale Carnegie "Personal Achievement Award". Since Fall, 1992, he has been the Director for the Center of Entrepreneurship at Clark Atlanta University; the only center of its type housed at a historically black college or university in the nation. His recent book, <u>Daily Motivations for African American Success</u> promises to be another best seller.

Dr. Dennis Kimbro spends much of his time traveling and speaking. He has addressed the Notre Dame football team and the Professional Golf Association in addition to appearing on the *Today Show* and *Larry King*. He has also been featured in <u>Success</u>, <u>Black Enterprise</u>, <u>Essence</u>, <u>The New York Times</u>, and <u>USA Today</u> on numerous occasions sharing the keys of success and achievement.

3806 Brandeis Court
Decatur, Georgia 30034
404-808-7696

THE P. KIMBRO GROUP, INC.

Mr. Andy Andrews
Lightning Crown Publishers
PO Box 17321
Nashville, Tennessee 37217

Dear Andy:

The power of persistence is true of all individuals who have carved their names onto the tablet of success. It is not so much brilliancy of intellect or talent or resources as it is persistency of effort and constancy of purpose that draws men and women to greatness. I have come to know first hand about the power of persistence.

On a late fall day, W. Clement Stone invited me to meet with him at his Chicago office. In the course of our meeting, Stone spoke of achievement, wealth and success. He detailed the rudiments of his philosophy, formed from his experience as one of the world's most successful businessmen. He explained that fortune and fame could be enjoyed by anyone willing to follow a specific formula. Then, dramatically and unexpectedly, Stone pulled out an unfinished manuscript and handed it to me. It was a draft of a book that Napoleon Hill, America's most prolific self-help writer and author of the phenomenal best seller, *Think and Grow Rich*, was preparing at the time of his death--*two decades ago!* Hill postulated it is no more difficult to aim high in life and achieve prosperity than it is to accept and live with poverty and misery. Just as I had studied successful black business people--what made them tick, what traits and qualities accounted for their success--Hill, too, had asked the exact question for blacks from all sectors of society: *How could Black Americans--or any group of people--pull themselves out of poverty and create wealth?* Hill had written nearly 100 pages on the subject, which turned out to be his last.

For the next five years, despite monetary hardship and periods of discontent, I saw in my mind's eye and held hopes of presenting Black America with a manual that embodied the principles of success and personal achievement. *Think and Grow Rich: A Black Choice* offers the same type of advice as the original and most popular self-help book ever written--but with a twist: *It is the first self-help book targeted to the African-American reader.*

"Learn How To Say 'I Can'!"

P. KIMBRO GROUP, INC.

A. Andrews
page 2.

Within his laboratory, I discovered a simple truth that is not only the core premise of self-help and motivation, but an acknowledged fact in the science of human behavior: Human beings are what they think they are. You can only be what you think you can be--*if you persist!*

So, the next time you encounter challenges or setbacks, remember that every failure or adversity carries with it the seed of an equivalent benefit. Begin to recognize that seed, plant it through action, *and stick to it!*

Sincerely,

Dennis P. Kimbro
The Legacy of Achievement

"Keep up the fires of thought,
and all will go well...
you fail in your thoughts or
you prevail in your thoughts
alone."

Thoreau

WILL CLARK
PROFESSIONAL BASEBALL PLAYER

…is one of the top players in Major League Baseball. Now with the Texas Rangers, he started his career with the San Francisco Giants.

When Will Clark stepped up to the plate for his first Major League at bat, it was April 8, 1986. Facing the rookie was perhaps one of the most feared fastballers of all time—Nolan Ryan. No one who was watching the game on television has forgotten what happened. On his first swing, Will hit a home run.

In the years since, Will has not slowed down. His numbers and leadership ability have been phenomenal. He is a perennial All-Star and is said to be one of the most gifted ball players of our generation.

Will has also worked very hard to get where he is. For years he has taken between 200 and 400 swings a day, rain or shine, and he has spent a lifetime developing his positive attitude.

I have known Will for some time now. He gives freely of himself to charitable causes and is always willing to help a friend. He is also a good example for those of us who face everyday challenges. He has a sense of humor about himself and the quiet confidence of a winner.

Will Clark
San Francisco Giants

Mr. Andy Andrews
P. O. Box 2761
Gulf Shores, AL 36547

Dear Andy,

When I was 14 years old, the All Star team that would represent New Orleans in the Babe Ruth World Series was being selected. The regular season had gone well for me and I was optimistic about my chances of being included.

The coach of the team had chosen all but the last two spots--and there were three of us left! The choice he had to make was between hitting versus speed. I was hoping he'd select hitting, which would swing the pick in my direction. If he decided to go with speed, I knew that I would be left out.

Since the purpose of this letter is to relate a disappointing experience in my life, you have probably already guessed the coach's decision. He chose speed (and not me!).

Disappointment is too small a word to fully describe how I felt at the time. To be honest, I was even a little embarrassed. But now, in retrospect, I can see that the episode probably had something to do with my success.

Even though I felt badly about being passed over, I went to work improving my skills. My father told me to learn from the experience and get better so that I would be chosen next time. "Don't leave them any option in the future," were his words.

That's exactly what I did. I practiced and worked harder than most of the other guys were willing to. And of that original group who made the All Star team, I'm the only one who made the majors.

Everyone hits roadblocks in their life, but the people who achieve great success in any profession are those who determine to keep practicing and get better. When Michael Jordan was cut from his high school basketball team, he knew he had to improve. The others who were cut more than likely quit.

When Joe Montana was benched at Notre Dame, he kept working. I have seen other athletes in similar situations give up. A winner never quits. Whether the playing field is athletics or business, the only loser is the person who decides that the struggle is too tough.

A challenge is the dividing line between winners and losers. Losers stay on the side of the line that figure the challenge is too big. Winners meet a challenge and go through it, over it, or around it.

Keep in mind, challenges guard all success. If you want the rewards, don't quit. Keep working and get better at what you do. And don't leave them any option in the future!

Your friend,

Will Clark

BILL HANNA
PRODUCER OF ANIMATION

…is co-founder and co-chairman of Hanna Barbera, Inc., producer of the world's largest library of animated entertainment. He and his partner, Joseph Barbera, have won seven Academy Awards and eight Emmy Awards.

Bill Hanna is a major force in the field of animation. With Joe Barbera, his partner of more than fifty years, Bill has created a lifetime of entertainment for us all.

Their first collaboration at MGM in 1938 became the immortal "Tom and Jerry". They won additional acclaim for making cartoon characters dance with Gene Kelly in the motion picture "Anchors Aweigh" and swim with Esther Williams in "Dangerous When Wet".

Hanna-Barbera produced the first ever animated prime time show— "The Flintstones" which aired for six years. Following that success were the additional series "The Jetsons", "Top Cat", and "The Adventures of Johnny Quest".

Bill Hanna will always be remembered for the creation of our most lovable cartoon stars, each with their own unmistakable voice and personality. As Bill, in his letter, tells of his failure to become what he most wanted, I couldn't help being a little grateful for that failure. Had he succeeded, we would never have seen Huckleberry Hound or Yogi Bear, Quick Draw McGraw, Augi Doggie, or Snooper and Blabber.

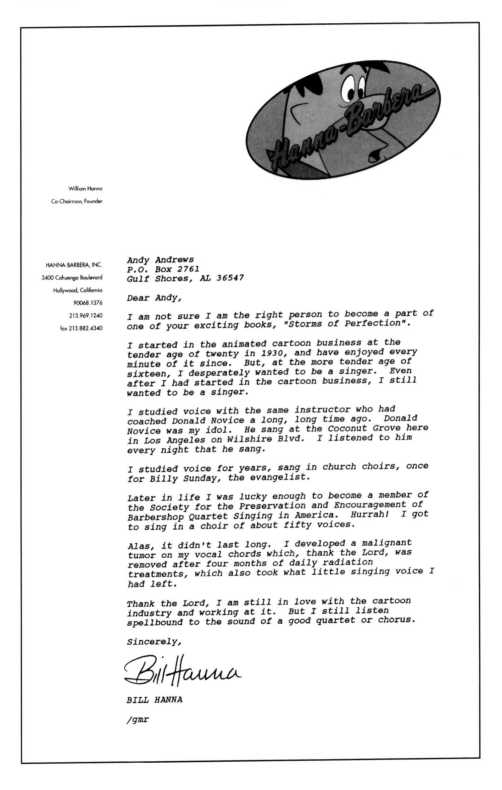

William Hanna
Co-Chairman, Founder

HANNA-BARBERA, INC.
3400 Cahuenga Boulevard
Hollywood, California
90068.1376
213.969.1240
fax 213.882.4340

Andy Andrews
P.O. Box 2761
Gulf Shores, AL 36547

Dear Andy,

I am not sure I am the right person to become a part of
one of your exciting books, "Storms of Perfection".

I started in the animated cartoon business at the
tender age of twenty in 1930, and have enjoyed every
minute of it since. But, at the more tender age of
sixteen, I desperately wanted to be a singer. Even
after I had started in the cartoon business, I still
wanted to be a singer.

I studied voice with the same instructor who had
coached Donald Novice a long, long time ago. Donald
Novice was my idol. He sang at the Coconut Grove here
in Los Angeles on Wilshire Blvd. I listened to him
every night that he sang.

I studied voice for years, sang in church choirs, once
for Billy Sunday, the evangelist.

Later in life I was lucky enough to become a member of
the Society for the Preservation and Encouragement of
Barbershop Quartet Singing in America. Hurrah! I got
to sing in a choir of about fifty voices.

Alas, it didn't last long. I developed a malignant
tumor on my vocal chords which, thank the Lord, was
removed after four months of daily radiation
treatments, which also took what little singing voice I
had left.

Thank the Lord, I am still in love with the cartoon
industry and working at it. But I still listen
spellbound to the sound of a good quartet or chorus.

Sincerely,

BILL HANNA

/gmr

ERMA BOMBECK
AUTHOR

...has been named to the list of the "25 Most Influential Women in America" by The World Almanac since 1979. She has also been featured on the cover of TIME Magazine.

Erma Bombeck has written a syndicated column for more than 700 newspapers for over 25 years. Her books are instant best sellers, each becoming bigger than the last so it is obvious that she is still gaining fans. I am one.

When I received the letter from Erma, I was thrilled. As a comedian, I have been intrigued by her style and consistency. She seems to be right on target every time. Her work is based on the everyday things we all see, but she points out the details that we often overlook—and she adds her comments to the mix.

I don't know if anyone has ever compared her work to that of Mark Twain or Will Rogers so I will do that here. There are very few people practicing any form of comedy or humor who appeal to all ages. In addition, there are not many who produce material that the whole family can enjoy. Erma Bombeck does. She is a national treasure.

Erma Bombeck

Dear Andy:

Your "charmed life" reference grabbed me.

If I lived such a charmed life, then how come
I didn't make it to Volume I of STORMS OF PERFECTION?

It's a great concept for a book because EVERY-
ONE can relate, I don't care who you are. Whenever
I speak at college commencements, I tell everyone
I'm up there and they're down there, not because of
my successes, but my failures. Then I proceed to
spin all of them off -- a comedy record album that
sold two copies in Beirut...a sitcom that lasted
about as long as a donut at our house...a Broadway
play that never saw Broadway...book signings where
I attracted two people: one who wanted directions
to the restroom and the other who wanted to buy the
desk.

What you have to tell yourself is, "I'm not a
failure. I failed at doing something." There's a
difference. I always remembered the words of a
crusty female naval officer who was noted for shaking
things up. She said, "A ship is safe in port...but
that's not where a ship was meant to be. Get out
there in rough waters." I believe if you're not
failing...you're not trying anything different.
You're not challenging yourself.

Personally and career-wise, it's been a corduroy
road. I've buried babies, lost parents, had cancer,
and worried over kids. The trick is to put it all
in perspective...and that's what I do for a living.

Erma Bombeck

Erma Bombeck

JOHN P. FOPPE
SPEAKER

...is a graduate of St. Louis University with a degree in communications. He is a professional inspirational speaker with The Zig Ziglar Corporation.

One day last Fall, I let my wife and several friends know that I had a sore throat. The discomfort I experienced talking and swallowing was about to ruin my day. Then, that afternoon, I met John. I still experience the occasional sore throat, but I am careful not to complain so loudly.

John learned at an early age that "our only real handicaps are those mental and emotional ones which prevent us from fully participating in life." The fourth of eight sons, John was born without arms.

He is an enthusiastic guy with a message for us all. In response to an emerging need for young motivational speakers who could address youth, John began to speak publicly when he was sixteen years old. Since that time, he has developed into a professional speaker addressing thousands of people from all walks of life.

John is constantly challenged to "walk his talk" and those who meet him are amazed at his ability to do so. He is a strong young man bringing a message of hope, patience, and perseverance.

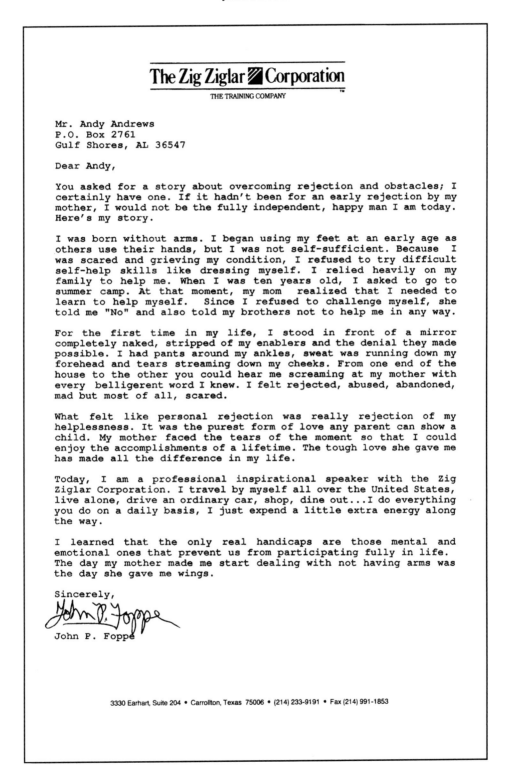

The Zig Ziglar ▨ Corporation
THE TRAINING COMPANY ™

Mr. Andy Andrews
P.O. Box 2761
Gulf Shores, AL 36547

Dear Andy,

You asked for a story about overcoming rejection and obstacles; I certainly have one. If it hadn't been for an early rejection by my mother, I would not be the fully independent, happy man I am today. Here's my story.

I was born without arms. I began using my feet at an early age as others use their hands, but I was not self-sufficient. Because I was scared and grieving my condition, I refused to try difficult self-help skills like dressing myself. I relied heavily on my family to help me. When I was ten years old, I asked to go to summer camp. At that moment, my mom realized that I needed to learn to help myself. Since I refused to challenge myself, she told me "No" and also told my brothers not to help me in any way.

For the first time in my life, I stood in front of a mirror completely naked, stripped of my enablers and the denial they made possible. I had pants around my ankles, sweat was running down my forehead and tears streaming down my cheeks. From one end of the house to the other you could hear me screaming at my mother with every belligerent word I knew. I felt rejected, abused, abandoned, mad but most of all, scared.

What felt like personal rejection was really rejection of my helplessness. It was the purest form of love any parent can show a child. My mother faced the tears of the moment so that I could enjoy the accomplishments of a lifetime. The tough love she gave me has made all the difference in my life.

Today, I am a professional inspirational speaker with the Zig Ziglar Corporation. I travel by myself all over the United States, live alone, drive an ordinary car, shop, dine out...I do everything you do on a daily basis, I just expend a little extra energy along the way.

I learned that the only real handicaps are those mental and emotional ones that prevent us from participating fully in life. The day my mother made me start dealing with not having arms was the day she gave me wings.

Sincerely,

John P. Foppe

3330 Earhart, Suite 204 • Carrollton, Texas 75006 • (214) 233-9191 • Fax (214) 991-1853

LEIGH STEINBERG
ATTORNEY

...is the country's leading sports attorney. He has been featured on television programs such as "60 Minutes" and "Lifestyles of the Rich and Famous" and magazines such as "Sports Illustrated" and "Success".

Leigh Steinberg's skill at the negotiation table was evident from the day he began his practice. In 1975, he worked out a then-record $650,000 contract for his first client, Steve Bartkowski. Then, in 1984, he negotiated what still stands as the largest contract ever recorded in professional sports when Steve Young signed a 40 million dollar deal with the USFL's Los Angeles Express.

Leigh's client roster reads like a "Who's Who" of professional sports and includes stars from football, baseball, basketball, and broadcasting. Besides Steve Young, they include Warren Moon, Troy Aikman, Jeff George, and Will Clark.

What distinguishes Leigh from others in his profession is his desire to make his clients more cognizant of their potential to influence people, particularly young people, and act as positive role models in today's society. While he has earned a reputation for getting great deals for his clients, Leigh insists that part of those deals require the player to give something back to a charitable organization. As a result, Leigh's clients have donated a total of over 35 million dollars to various charities and scholarship funds across the nation.

LAW OFFICES

STEINBERG & MOORAD
A PROFESSIONAL CORPORATION

500 NEWPORT CENTER DRIVE
SUITE 820
NEWPORT BEACH, CALIFORNIA 92660
(714) 720-8700
FAX (714) 720-1331

109 PANORAMIC WAY
BERKELEY, CALIFORNIA 94704
(510) 848-0216
FAX (510) 848-2516

2737 DUNLEER PLACE
LOS ANGELES, CALIFORNIA 90064
(310) 838-2917

LEIGH STEINBERG
JEFFREY S. MOORAD

DAVID L. DUNN
SCOTT G. PARKER

Andy Andrews
P.O. Box 2761
Gulf Shores, AL 36547

Dear Andy:

I fell into a career of Sports and Entertainment Law in a totally unplanned way. I had served as a dorm counselor in an undergraduate dorm as a means of working my way through law school at the University of California at Berkeley. One of the students in the dorm was Steve Bartkowski, a quarterback who was selected as the very first pick in the 1975 National Football League draft by the Atlanta Falcons.

I graduated from law school in January 1974 and travelled around the world until early 1975. Before I had a chance to accept a job with the Alameda County District Attorney's office, Bartkowski asked me to represent him in his contract negotiations with the Falcons.

What an incredible experience. We were able to negotiate the largest rookie contract in the history of football which made headlines all across the country. We were greeted by crowds of fans, banners and television crews at the airport.

I established a law practice based on athletes serving as charitable and community figures, setting up programs that retraced their roots. Behind all that glamour and promise the reality of my situation was much different. My office consisted of a card table in a small room in my parent's home. I had no secretary or help of any sort. I answered my own phone and spent much of my time typing letters and going to the copy store. I lived with my parents, drove a beat-up 1967 Ford Pinto and didn't even have my own credit cards.

From June 1975 through January 1977 I did not sign another top draftee. Other agents were giving money to players to induce them to sign representation contracts. I had no desire to compete in that way. Many athletes were turned off by my charitable requirements. Soon the expenses of even my modest operation far exceeded my income. I had run through my father's credit line, my phone lines were about to be cut off and my operation closed. But my work with Steve Bartkowski convinced me there was a real opportunity to do good in the world with athletes serving as models.

So I borrowed $300.00 from Steve Bartkowski, flew to Atlanta, rented a car using Bartkowski's credit cards and drove to the University of Georgia where I met with a highly rated offensive lineman by the name of Joel "Cowboy" Parrish. I signed him as a client. Joel, along with teammate Mike "Moonpie" Wilson, soon signed a lucrative contract with the Toronto Argonauts of the Canadian Football League. He paid me a large enough fee to keep going, and I've spent the last 18 years representing star athletes.

The key to finding strength in the face of adversity is to believe strongly that you can make a real difference in the world and to believe strongly that there is never an excuse to give up.

I always try to keep in perspective the fact that not withstanding how daunting our problems are, they are minor and easy compared with people who live with severe illnesses or physical disabilities, or don't have enough to eat or are victims of war or dictatorship.

We are blessed to live in a free country and there is never an excuse for giving up.

Sincerely,

Leigh Steinberg

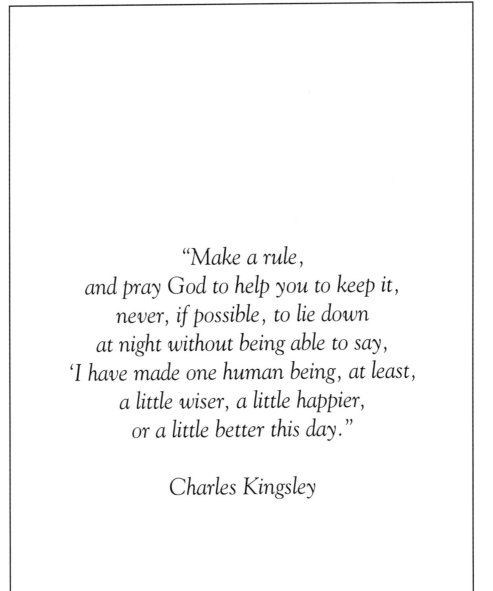

"Make a rule,
and pray God to help you to keep it,
never, if possible, to lie down
at night without being able to say,
'I have made one human being, at least,
a little wiser, a little happier,
or a little better this day."

Charles Kingsley

DR. ROBERT H. SCHULLER
MINISTER/AUTHOR

...is the Crystal Cathedral's founding pastor. He is also the author of more than thirty books, five of which have appeared on the New York Times best-seller list.

Born in Alton, Iowa in 1926, Robert Harold Schuller knew all his life that he wanted to become a minister. He fulfilled that dream in 1950. Today, Dr. Schuller reaches millions around the world with his "Hour of Power" ministry televised live from the Crystal Cathedral in Garden Grove, California.

Dr. Schuller came to Garden Grove in 1955 to found the Reformed Church of America's congregation there. With his wife, Arvella, as the organist and $500 in assets, he rented the Orange Drive-in Theater and conducted Sunday services from the roof of the snack bar.

The "Hour of Power" is the highest rated religious program in the country. In 1989, Dr. Schuller became the first non-Soviet pastor ever to be invited to speak on Soviet television and is now seen every Sunday morning throughout the former Soviet Union.

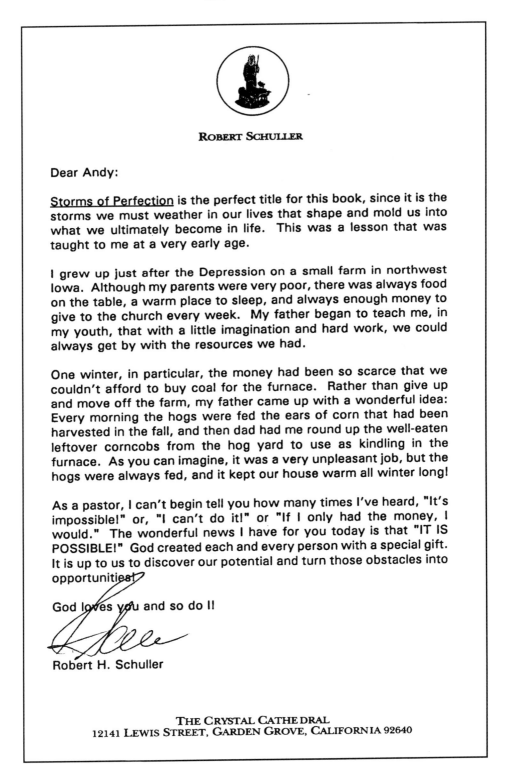

ROBERT SCHULLER

Dear Andy:

<u>Storms of Perfection</u> is the perfect title for this book, since it is the storms we must weather in our lives that shape and mold us into what we ultimately become in life. This was a lesson that was taught to me at a very early age.

I grew up just after the Depression on a small farm in northwest Iowa. Although my parents were very poor, there was always food on the table, a warm place to sleep, and always enough money to give to the church every week. My father began to teach me, in my youth, that with a little imagination and hard work, we could always get by with the resources we had.

One winter, in particular, the money had been so scarce that we couldn't afford to buy coal for the furnace. Rather than give up and move off the farm, my father came up with a wonderful idea: Every morning the hogs were fed the ears of corn that had been harvested in the fall, and then dad had me round up the well-eaten leftover corncobs from the hog yard to use as kindling in the furnace. As you can imagine, it was a very unpleasant job, but the hogs were always fed, and it kept our house warm all winter long!

As a pastor, I can't begin tell you how many times I've heard, "It's impossible!" or, "I can't do it!" or "If I only had the money, I would." The wonderful news I have for you today is that "IT IS POSSIBLE!" God created each and every person with a special gift. It is up to us to discover our potential and turn those obstacles into opportunities!

God loves you and so do I!

Robert H. Schuller

THE CRYSTAL CATHEDRAL
12141 LEWIS STREET, GARDEN GROVE, CALIFORNIA 92640

THE STATLER BROTHERS
ENTERTAINERS

...have won more awards than any group in the history of country music. This includes three Grammys, 47 Music City News Awards, and the Country Music Association's Vocal Group of the Year award eleven times.

I was about to appear on "The Statler Brothers Show". After the commercial break, the guys were to introduce me. It was then that I chose to ask them for a letter. Harold said, "Well, if we say 'no', you'll probably do a lousy job here tonight...so I guess the answer is 'yes'." I knew that it would be.

When you see the Statlers on stage, you are seeing them as they are. Harold is always cutting up, Don is usually trying to quiet Harold, Jimmy is laughing at Don trying to quiet Harold, and Phil is just plain quiet. They are all great guys.

The Statlers have dedicated their careers to making other people happy. Long after some groups have made their mark and folded their tents, the Statlers keep on rolling. They are superstars of country music, yet their feet remain firmly on the ground. The men Kurt Vonnegut called "America's Poets" still live in their hometown of 22,000 with their offices located in their old elementary school.

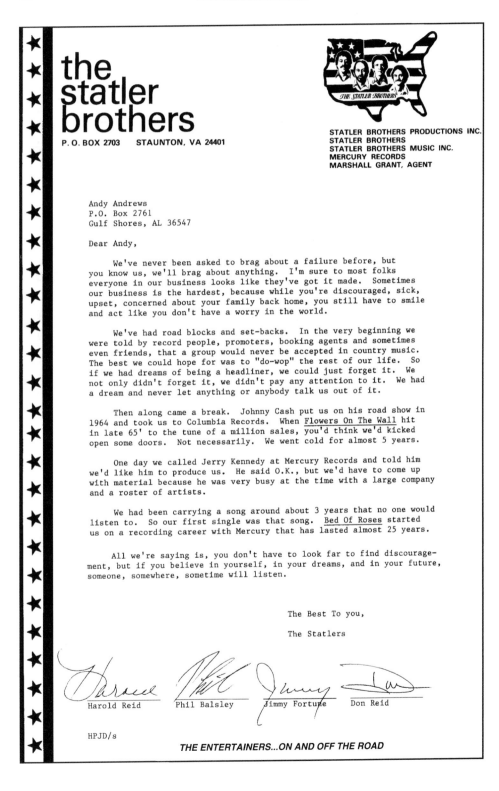

the statler brothers

P. O. BOX 2703   STAUNTON, VA 24401

STATLER BROTHERS PRODUCTIONS INC.
STATLER BROTHERS
STATLER BROTHERS MUSIC INC.
MERCURY RECORDS
MARSHALL GRANT, AGENT

Andy Andrews
P.O. Box 2761
Gulf Shores, AL 36547

Dear Andy,

We've never been asked to brag about a failure before, but you know us, we'll brag about anything. I'm sure to most folks everyone in our business looks like they've got it made. Sometimes our business is the hardest, because while you're discouraged, sick, upset, concerned about your family back home, you still have to smile and act like you don't have a worry in the world.

We've had road blocks and set-backs. In the very beginning we were told by record people, promoters, booking agents and sometimes even friends, that a group would never be accepted in country music. The best we could hope for was to "do-wop" the rest of our life. So if we had dreams of being a headliner, we could just forget it. We not only didn't forget it, we didn't pay any attention to it. We had a dream and never let anything or anybody talk us out of it.

Then along came a break. Johnny Cash put us on his road show in 1964 and took us to Columbia Records. When Flowers On The Wall hit in late 65' to the tune of a million sales, you'd think we'd kicked open some doors. Not necessarily. We went cold for almost 5 years.

One day we called Jerry Kennedy at Mercury Records and told him we'd like him to produce us. He said O.K., but we'd have to come up with material because he was very busy at the time with a large company and a roster of artists.

We had been carrying a song around about 3 years that no one would listen to. So our first single was that song. Bed Of Roses started us on a recording career with Mercury that has lasted almost 25 years.

All we're saying is, you don't have to look far to find discouragement, but if you believe in yourself, in your dreams, and in your future, someone, somewhere, sometime will listen.

The Best To you,

The Statlers

Harold Reid   Phil Balsley   Jimmy Fortune   Don Reid

HPJD/s

THE ENTERTAINERS...ON AND OFF THE ROAD

BOBBY BOWDEN
COLLEGE FOOTBALL COACH

...won his first National Championship in 1993. He is the only coach in history to put together six consecutive 10-win seasons. He also owns the all-time Bowl winning percentage of .781 (12-3-1), the best ever in college football.

Bobby Bowden is a living legend in collegiate football. Three years after walking onto the Florida State University campus, he took one of the nation's worst football teams to within one game of a National Championship. He has achieved an incredible winning record, now a tradition, against some of the nation's toughest schedules.

On and off the field, Coach Bowden has a charm and humor that attracts everyone. Respect, honor, love, sincerity, class, and charisma link him to such greats as Bryant, Stagg, and Warner.

When Bobby Bowden went to Tallahassee in 1976, he promised a winning program. He has been a man of his word. In his eighteen years as head coach of the Seminoles, FSU has been to fifteen Bowl Games and has finished in the top four for the last seven years.

Because of his character and style, Coach Bowden is more than just a regional success. He is a national figure who draws praise as an inspiration to us all.

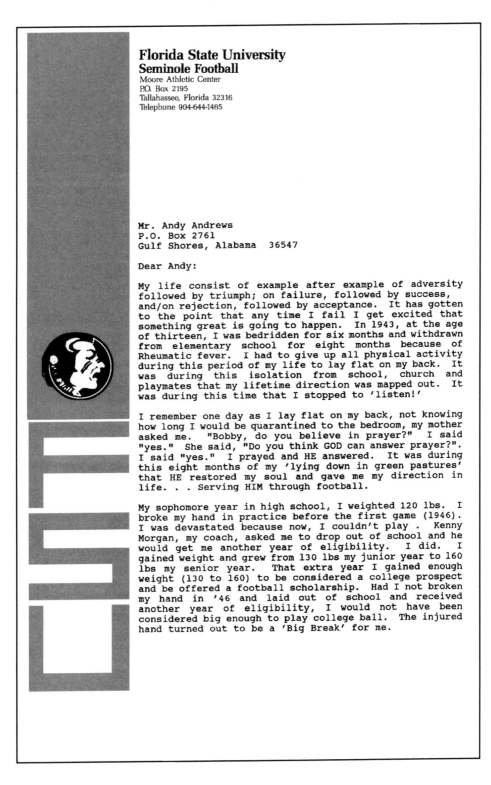

Florida State University
Seminole Football
Moore Athletic Center
P.O. Box 2195
Tallahassee, Florida 32316
Telephone 904-644-1465

Mr. Andy Andrews
P.O. Box 2761
Gulf Shores, Alabama   36547

Dear Andy:

My life consist of example after example of adversity
followed by triumph; on failure, followed by success,
and/on rejection, followed by acceptance. It has gotten
to the point that any time I fail I get excited that
something great is going to happen. In 1943, at the age
of thirteen, I was bedridden for six months and withdrawn
from elementary school for eight months because of
Rheumatic fever. I had to give up all physical activity
during this period of my life to lay flat on my back. It
was during this isolation from school, church and
playmates that my lifetime direction was mapped out. It
was during this time that I stopped to 'listen!'

I remember one day as I lay flat on my back, not knowing
how long I would be quarantined to the bedroom, my mother
asked me. "Bobby, do you believe in prayer?" I said
"yes." She said, "Do you think GOD can answer prayer?".
I said "yes." I prayed and HE answered. It was during
this eight months of my 'lying down in green pastures'
that HE restored my soul and gave me my direction in
life. . . Serving HIM through football.

My sophomore year in high school, I weighted 120 lbs. I
broke my hand in practice before the first game (1946).
I was devastated because now, I couldn't play . Kenny
Morgan, my coach, asked me to drop out of school and he
would get me another year of eligibility. I did. I
gained weight and grew from 130 lbs my junior year to 160
lbs my senior year. That extra year I gained enough
weight (130 to 160) to be considered a college prospect
and be offered a football scholarship. Had I not broken
my hand in '46 and laid out of school and received
another year of eligibility, I would not have been
considered big enough to play college ball. The injured
hand turned out to be a 'Big Break' for me.

Andy Andrews
Page 2

Every job I applied for in coaching, I was 'rejected'.
I never got a coaching job I applied for. (1) South
Georgia College, (2) Samford University, (3) West
Virginia University and (4) Florida State University,
all, out of the blue, called me and said "We want you as
our coach." Darn if God didn't get me better jobs than
the ones I applied for and was turned down. It all began
back there in 1943 (Rheumatic fever) when I stopped to
'listen' to God and my mother.

My best to you and good luck with your new book **STORMS OF
PERFECTION II.**

Sincerely,

BOBBY BOWDEN
Head Football Coach

BB/sh

Psalms 42:1

"The greater the difficulty,
the greater the glory."

Cicero

DANITA ALLEN
EDITOR

...is the founding editor of COUNTRY AMERICA MAGAZINE *– now with over one million subscribers, it is the fastest growing magazine in the United States.*

I love to talk to Danita on the phone. Some time ago, I began writing a monthly column for COUNTRY AMERICA MAGAZINE. The stories are all sequels one to the other; all about the people of Sawyerton Springs, Alabama. My editor for these pieces is *the* editor...Danita.

We have become great friends, talking and laughing about why a word was changed or deleted. In fact, there is probably no one I would rather talk to on the phone – except when she calls to tell me that my column is late!

Danita joined Meredith Corporation, the publisher of COUNTRY AMERICA in 1980. She had previously been a communications instructor with the University of Missouri College of Agriculture for three years.

Danita and her husband Greg currently live on a small farm outside of Des Moines, Iowa with their three children and a changing menagerie of horses, donkeys, cattle, sheep, chickens, dogs and cats.

1716 Locust Street
Des Moines, Iowa 50309-3023

Dear Andy,

In your letter, you speculated many people are probably under the impression I lead a charmed life. I do! I get to meet and interview country singers and other entertainers like you! What fun!

You asked about failures or rejections I've experienced. Honestly, there haven't been many. At least, I don't look at my experiences as failures or rejections. Maybe that's key.

Let me tell you how a Missouri farm girl who grew up milking cows came to be the founding editor of a magazine that is now on the top 100 list of magazines by circulation size and was recently named the hottest magazine in America by *Adweek* magazine.

I must have learned how to work hard from my parents, who worked from dawn to dusk every day except Sunday, when they still had to milk the cows. Although I don't remember ever feeling poor, we were probably land rich and cash poor. We had nice clothes, but we sewed all of them ourselves—even underwear and swimsuits—because that was cheaper than buying them.

My parents encouraged us to do our best and to try new things. We learned about winning—and not winning—first in 4-H, where we showed everything from calves to vegetables and sewing projects. Later, we entered spelling, writing and speaking contests.

With the aid of a scholarship, a part-time job and help from my folks, I went to college. While there, I gained valuable experience by volunteering to work on my college newspaper. That experience gave me the edge I needed to win an internship at the top agricultural magazine in the country, *Successful Farming*.

While at *Successful Farming,* I ran into the biggest failure of my career, although I didn't look at it as *my* failure at the time. During the mid-80s, I proposed to Meredith Corporation, our publisher, that it should start a new magazine on country life called *Country Place*. While working at my full-time job, I was also researching, planning, writing long lists of story ideas and actually mocking up that magazine. I presented the magazine idea, was given enough funding for additional research, but then was eventually denied funds for actual testing of the idea. So *Country Place* died. I guess that was a failure.

The good news is that when The Nashville Network was looking for someone to publish a program guide they approached Meredith. Company executives remembered the country life magazine idea and thought that rather than publishing a small guide, perhaps the country life and country music ideas could be combined. Because I had proposed the initial country life magazine, I had the opportunity to develop the concept for *Country America* as well. The company liked my concept and development work well enough to hire me as editor. So that earlier country magazine failure led directly to my current success.

I always believe that if God closes one door, he'll open another. I'm thankful for the doors he's opened for me.

All the Best,

Danita Allen
Editor

JOHN F. NORTHCOTT
WORLD WAR II POW

...was a Bataan-Corregidor survivor. A prisoner of war for 43 months, he was liberated in Japan upon surrender in 1945.

I feel privileged to know John Northcott and to have spent time with him and his family. His story is as horrifying as any I have come across and yet, his attitude today is one of gratefulness and joy.

When I received John's letter, I read and re-read it several times. I called friends and read it to them over the phone. In every case, they were moved. His words are not for the faint of heart. His story is a graphic account of one man's hell on earth and the struggle to survive.

As a person who has never experienced challenges of this type, I can only marvel at the courage and incredible will to overcome that John must surely possess. After reading his letter, finding problems in everyday circumstances is almost embarrassing. As an example of the ability to find light in any situation, John Northcott's very life is a wealth of encouragement and inspiration.

JOHN F. NORTHCOTT

805 Oak Drive
Leesburg, Florida 34748-4322

Mr. Andy Andrews
P. O. Box 2761
Gulf Shores, AL 36547

Dear Andy,

It was not difficult to choose the toughest storm in my life. Though it ended almost 50 years ago, the memories are with me still. Since you asked me to give a detailed account of my experience, I will do so here for the first time in my life outside of family and friends. I must warn you, however, that this is not a pretty story, but every word of it is the truth. I will not write about things I heard; I will only commit to this paper the instances I experienced first-hand.

It was early morning, December 7, 1941. I was on the 4 to 8 watch on my first ship, the USS Vaga-YT-116. We watched as the Admiral's Barge pulled alongside. Our skipper was handed a written message that the Japanese had attacked Pearl Harbor. We were instructed to assume war condition.

We immediately painted the whole ship gray, removed all uprights and awnings that might affect vision, and within three hours were steaming toward Cavile Naval Base in Manila for further assignment. Less than fifty yards of the harbor, we were attacked for the first time in what, for me, would be a long war.

Several months later, we were ordered to report to MacArthur's command at Corregidor. There I was assigned to the 4th marines because I was a qualified 50 caliber machine gunner. At this time, Corregidor was being bombed almost 24 hours a day everyday.

Meanwhile, our boys on Bataan were fighting and holding--beating the Japanese bad. But after six weeks with no reinforcements, our troops were in dire shape. Food was getting scarce. They had killed and eaten all the water buffalo, monkeys, dogs, snakes and horses that were on the island. Most of the troops were sick with malaria and dysentery and they had no medicine at all.

We made runs between Bataan and Corregidor bringing supplies but by late February of that year it was obvious that our guys were too sick and weak to be able to fight. Still, they held out for five months.

Finally, at about 2 AM on the 10th of April, we received word to proceed to Bataan and pick up as many survivors as we could from the ocean. These were troops who had retreated and tried to swim to Corregidor rather than surrender to the Japanese who were advancing.

It was a hellish nightmare. Everything was blowing up in huge fireballs all around us. We picked up so many men from the ocean that we were in danger of sinking ourselves. It was a heart rending experience as there were so many men still in the water. They were yelling to be picked up and calling out their names and addresses, hoping we'd remember them for their families back home.

We were helpless to help them. The only option we had was to return to Corregidor, unload as fast as we would, and go back to pick up some more. We were not allowed to return, however, because the area had been overrun. That was one low and painful day that I have never gotten over.

On the evening of May 10, our officers called us to order and told us to destroy all weapons--Corregidor had surrendered. About 30,000 of us marched down to the surrender point. It was an area of concrete with no shade and one water spigot for all of us. We stayed in this place for three weeks during which time they did not feed us. The water line was 24 hours a day. Once they did open the tunnel where food was kept on Corregidor and let us scavenge all we could get for an hour. Everyone got enough to keep from starving.

Next, we were marched to a condemned prison that had been built in 1800 by the Spainairds. The prison, Bilibid, was where we got our first solid meal--watery boiled rice with small worms floating in it. Some tried picking them off, but you either ate it or went hungry.

There was no running water in this place and the men all had malaria and dysentery. For the first few weeks, we were burying about 100 to 150 men daily.

I remember one fellow was buried three different times. He would be in the makeshift morgue and every time we put him in the ground, he would somehow come to. He almost didn't make it the third time because we had shoveled dirt over him, but darned if he didn't raise his arm!

In Bilibid, the Japanese used us for work details. Whenever they asked for so many men in a work party, a few of us volunteered no matter what the work was. That way we could steal food at every opportunity. We would turn the food over to our doctors at the hospital. We had to hide the food because if you were caught, they would beat you with rifle butts in the head, back, or legs. Those that were caught usually became a permanent hospital patient or crippled. I had two close calls this way and still cannot get over the fact that I was not caught.

Another punishment that I personally witnessed was known as the water treatment. One prisoner was accused of trading with a civilian outside the prison while on a work detail. They beat him until he was half conscious and then spread him spread-eagle. A guard stood on each hand and leg while another put a water hose down his throat. When the water was turned on full blast, he died.

After what seemed like a lifetime in Bilibid, we were transferred to Cabanatuan Prison. That place was worse than anything I had ever seen. We lived in bamboo shacks with bamboo floors. The flies, insects, and mosquitoes were so thick you did not want to open your mouth.

We were divided into groups of ten with the condition that if one of us escaped or was missing, the other nine would be shot. At one point, one guy did try to escape and was caught. The next day, the other nine were made to dig their own hole and line up. The officer in charge came over to the young kid who had tried to escape and asked if he had anything to say. The kid looked him straight in the eye and spit in his face. The officer was so mad that he shot him on the spot and then they shot the others.

Another time, a prisoner was caught talking to civilians outside camp while on a work detail. He tried to explain that he was only trading for food, but the Japanese officer would not listen. They took him back to camp and called us all out to watch as the officer made him kneel and cut his head off. They then placed his head on a post and set it in the middle of the camp for everyone to see. It stayed there for three days before they took it off and had it buried. This happed twice that I witnessed.

Things were getting bad in Japan due to our continued air raids. They were conscripting old men and young children in the military. These people were coming from their factories. To replace them, the Japanese decided to use American prisoners.

When we boarded the ship to be taken to Japan, they put 1,300 of us in one hold. The name of the ship was the Nissei Maru---a cattle vessel. We were so packed, standing, that when a man died, he would not be able to fall down. Finally, they made us sit down by squatting in a position you would be in if you were rowing.

They lowered two buckets in the hold for toilets and also lowered rice that way once a day. It was not long before the hold became a stinking, nauseating place. The buckets had overflowed because everyone was sick. Most of the men who could no longer move were laying in their own feces and urine and didn't care. They were waiting to die.

We each ate a couple of tablespoons of raw rice every 2 or 3 days. Water was just as scarce and efforts to get more was to no avail. Everyone was starving. Three men and one officer were caught and hanged by the prisoners for cutting the veins of other prisoners and drinking their blood at night. We threw our dead overboard daily and 42 days later, when we reached Japan, there were 400 of us left.

In Japan, we were not allowed to possess any Japanese items. This was a capital offense. Any American caught with Japanese money or goods of any kind was beheaded on the spot.

In early August, we started seeing dogfights between Japanese and American planes over our camp. Then one day, we could no longer work in our factory---our planes had bombed it to the ground. Soon, leaflets were dropped giving Japan 24 hours to surrender. A couple of days later, we felt a shock that knocked everything off the shelves and shook the barracks. We knew it was not an earthquake, but the guards told us nothing.

Andy, you know that this is the end of the story. Japan did surrender within days of the atomic blast. When we were liberated, I weighed 65 pounds, but considered myself lucky. Of the 30,000 of us who had been captured 43 months earlier, only 3,000 of us had survived the prison camps.

Many people who read this letter might find it impossible to believe that anything positive could have possibly come out of these experiences. But the storm so long ago has given me a gratefulness of little things that others do not have. And that storm has given my life perspective.

I watch people who let a headache ruin their day. Things like a flat tire, busy phone lines, and crying babies give some people ulcers. Marital spats, financial troubles, and cancelled flights give people high blood pressure. But I have to tell you. To me, those things are no big deal. I'm just happy to be here!

Sincerely,

John F. Northcott

John F. Northcott
U.S.N. Retired

MONTY HALL
TELEVISION PERSONALITY

...is best known for his twenty-two years as the popular host of "Lets Make A Deal!".

For years, I knew exactly where my father would be when lunch time rolled around. He would be glued to the television watching "Lets Make A Deal!". Dad always made fun of the way some of the people dressed, but I still suspect he would have stood around in a garbage bag with grapes on his head if he'd had a chance at Door Number three. Of course, right in the middle of it all was Monty Hall.

Considering the show ran for twenty-two years, it's no wonder that we remember Monty best for "Lets Make A Deal!" It is for this and many other accomplishments that Monty Hall was awarded his own star on Hollywood's Walk of Fame.

Equally important is Monty's life away from television. He travels the world speaking and performing for countless charities. He also serves on the board of many organizations who do work for disease control and better hospital care. His charitable and philanthropic activities have brought him over 500 awards and a great deal of personal satisfaction.

monty hall

Andy Andrews
P.O. Box 2761
Gulf Shores, Alabama 36547

Dear Andy:

In reading your book, STORMS OF PERFECTION, I realized
that a great many people in this world have had to
overcome adversity to get to where they are. My story
is not much different.

I was raised in Winnipeg, Canada, during the Depression;
and when I finished high school at a very early age,
my family couldn't afford to send me on to college.
So I went to work in the family store as a delivery
boy and saved enough money to go back for two years
of college. After my second year, I found that I
was tapped out and could not continue. So I went
to work in a wholesale clothing emporium. If I
thought I had it bad at my father's store, this
experience was a nightmare.

I worked for a cruel boss who humiliated me at
every turn. He delighted in following me around
the plant as I swept and washed the floor, pointing
out a particle that I had missed here and there. On
one particular day, when he demeaned me with some
remark, I came home crestfallen and told my mother
what had happened. My mother, a former schoolteacher
and entertainer, was a brilliang woman. She sat me
down and recited Rudyard Kipling's "If" ...

> "If you can keep your head when all about
> you
> Are losing theirs and blaming it on you"...

Then she told me of the disappointments she had had
in her life and how she overcame them with perseverance
and determination. I believe this pep talk helped
change my life around.

I quit my job, found another source of income and a
benefactor and went back to college. I received a
Bachelor of Science degree, was elected student body
president and paid off all my debts by working at a

Andy Andrews   - 2 -

radio station at night. Any rejections I had in the
broadcasting business from that point on were a lot
easier to accept and overcome because of what I
learned in my youth. That is why when young people
today seek out my advice, I tell them they need
three things: desire, courage and luck. The desire,
of course, precedes everything, because you must
want your goal very badly. Then you have to have the
courage to stick it out until that great moment comes
when desire and courage intersect with luck. I believe
it was the late Branch Rickey of the Brooklyn Dodgers
who said it best: "Luck is the residue of desire."

Well, Andy, I have a few more of these "storms" I have
overcome, but I will wait to put them in your editions
IV, V and VI.

                              All my best,

                              Monty Hall

MH:ji

"There are two kinds of
discontent in this world,
the discontent that works,
and the discontent that wrings its hands.
The first gets what it wants,
and the second loses what it has.
There's no cure for the first but success,
and there's no cure at all for the second."

Gordon Graham

CHI CHI RODRIGUEZ
PROFESSIONAL GOLFER

...was inducted into the PGA World Golf Hall of Fame in 1992. He has won the Digital Seniors Classic for three consecutive years.

At the age of twelve, Chi Chi scored a 67 and knew he was destined to play the game that was to become his life...golf. Since his early days in Puerto Rico, Chi Chi has put a lot of himself into this intense game that often produces stress in those of us who play on weekends. From the acting of a matador, with his club as a sword, to his quips about his respected peers, he is always fun to watch.

Chi Chi also sets aside countless hours to spend at his pride and joy...the Chi Chi Rodriguez Youth Foundation. The foundation is located in Clearwater, Florida and is a home for troubled and abused youngsters. Chi Chi himself calls the children for progress reports and to offer words of encouragement.

I have followed Chi Chi's career for many years and have been drawn to his personality and skill. It is gratifying to know that on top of everything else, he has a heart as big as the sky.

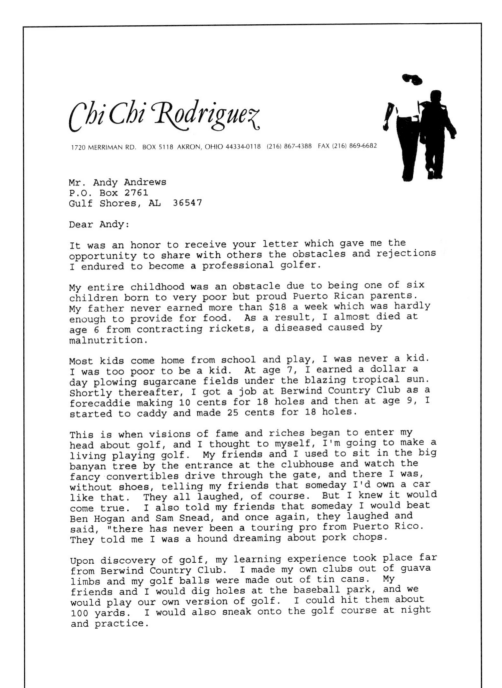

Chi Chi Rodriguez

1720 MERRIMAN RD. BOX 5118 AKRON, OHIO 44334-0118 (216) 867-4388 FAX (216) 869-6682

Mr. Andy Andrews
P.O. Box 2761
Gulf Shores, AL 36547

Dear Andy:

It was an honor to receive your letter which gave me the
opportunity to share with others the obstacles and rejections
I endured to become a professional golfer.

My entire childhood was an obstacle due to being one of six
children born to very poor but proud Puerto Rican parents.
My father never earned more than $18 a week which was hardly
enough to provide for food. As a result, I almost died at
age 6 from contracting rickets, a diseased caused by
malnutrition.

Most kids come home from school and play, I was never a kid.
I was too poor to be a kid. At age 7, I earned a dollar a
day plowing sugarcane fields under the blazing tropical sun.
Shortly thereafter, I got a job at Berwind Country Club as a
forecaddie making 10 cents for 18 holes and then at age 9, I
started to caddy and made 25 cents for 18 holes.

This is when visions of fame and riches began to enter my
head about golf, and I thought to myself, I'm going to make a
living playing golf. My friends and I used to sit in the big
banyan tree by the entrance at the clubhouse and watch the
fancy convertibles drive through the gate, and there I was,
without shoes, telling my friends that someday I'd own a car
like that. They all laughed, of course. But I knew it would
come true. I also told my friends that someday I would beat
Ben Hogan and Sam Snead, and once again, they laughed and
said, "there has never been a touring pro from Puerto Rico.
They told me I was a hound dreaming about pork chops.

Upon discovery of golf, my learning experience took place far
from Berwind Country Club. I made my own clubs out of guava
limbs and my golf balls were made out of tin cans. My
friends and I would dig holes at the baseball park, and we
would play our own version of golf. I could hit them about
100 yards. I would also sneak onto the golf course at night
and practice.

During my two years in the Army, I was trying out for an Army baseball team, and watched a former major leaguer take his cuts. I knew then I could never play baseball. So the answer was golf. But my dad told me, "You forget that golf. No Puerto Rican has ever made it." That's all I thought about and was determined to show him.

One day in school the teacher mentioned the Gulf of Mexico; and I asked if it was spelled "golf" or "gulf." She said there is no such thing as "golf." I told her that someday I will be making a lot money doing "GOLF." She said, "sit down."

Once I arrived on the PGA Tour, my humorous antics were not welcomed by many of the players and as a result, I was fined and warned by the PGA for conduct "unbecoming a professional." But my most devastating experience was when my idol Arnold Palmer criticized me at the 1964 Masters for my antics. I went to the locker room and cried.

Even though I came from a very poor background and received little encouragement toward golf from family, friends, and peers, I am proof that a positive self-image paired with a positive attitude can work wonders.

Sincerely,

"Chichi"

Chi Chi Rodriguez

"*People do not lack strength;*
they lack will."

Victor Hugo

HARVEY MACKAY
AUTHOR/
BUSINESSMAN

...is Chairman and Chief Executive Officer of Mackay Envelope Corporation. He is the author of SWIM WITH THE SHARKS WITHOUT BEING EATEN ALIVE which was on the New York Times Best Seller List for fifty-four weeks.

I talked with Harvey on the phone one afternoon in Minneapolis and smiled the whole time. He has an engaging personality and a wonderful way of putting his ideas across. At one point, he told me that "if you give the public something that is used every day and provide it at a reasonable cost, you will have a successful business."

That is exactly what Harvey did in 1959 when he founded Mackay Envelope Corporation, a business that now manufactures over ten million envelopes per day. And who better to write a book about dealing with businessmen than a successful businessman!

Following his first book, which sold over four million copies, Harvey met equal success with BEWARE THE MAN WHO OFFERS YOU HIS SHIRT and SHARKPROOF: GET THE JOB YOU WANT, KEEP THE JOB YOU LOVE. These books also became national best sellers within weeks.

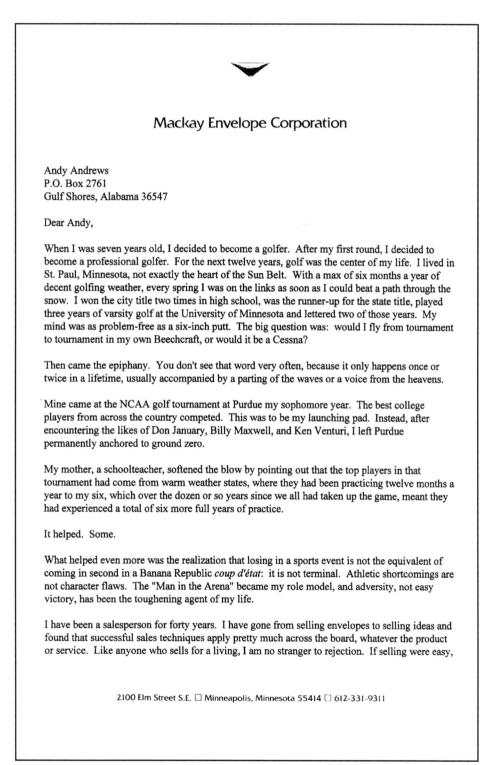

Mackay Envelope Corporation

Andy Andrews
P.O. Box 2761
Gulf Shores, Alabama 36547

Dear Andy,

When I was seven years old, I decided to become a golfer. After my first round, I decided to become a professional golfer. For the next twelve years, golf was the center of my life. I lived in St. Paul, Minnesota, not exactly the heart of the Sun Belt. With a max of six months a year of decent golfing weather, every spring I was on the links as soon as I could beat a path through the snow. I won the city title two times in high school, was the runner-up for the state title, played three years of varsity golf at the University of Minnesota and lettered two of those years. My mind was as problem-free as a six-inch putt. The big question was: would I fly from tournament to tournament in my own Beechcraft, or would it be a Cessna?

Then came the epiphany. You don't see that word very often, because it only happens once or twice in a lifetime, usually accompanied by a parting of the waves or a voice from the heavens.

Mine came at the NCAA golf tournament at Purdue my sophomore year. The best college players from across the country competed. This was to be my launching pad. Instead, after encountering the likes of Don January, Billy Maxwell, and Ken Venturi, I left Purdue permanently anchored to ground zero.

My mother, a schoolteacher, softened the blow by pointing out that the top players in that tournament had come from warm weather states, where they had been practicing twelve months a year to my six, which over the dozen or so years since we all had taken up the game, meant they had experienced a total of six more full years of practice.

It helped. Some.

What helped even more was the realization that losing in a sports event is not the equivalent of coming in second in a Banana Republic *coup d'état*: it is not terminal. Athletic shortcomings are not character flaws. The "Man in the Arena" became my role model, and adversity, not easy victory, has been the toughening agent of my life.

I have been a salesperson for forty years. I have gone from selling envelopes to selling ideas and found that successful sales techniques apply pretty much across the board, whatever the product or service. Like anyone who sells for a living, I am no stranger to rejection. If selling were easy,

2100 Elm Street S.E. □ Minneapolis, Minnesota 55414 □ 612-331-9311 who would need salespeople? It would be the low bid meeting specs every time, and insurance policies would jump off the shelves into customers' laps.

I have learned that in order to increase the number of my successes, I have had to accept an increase in the number of my failures. I think any success worth having is like a 100 rung ladder. There's no use trying to jump on in the middle; take it as a bottom to top proposition, one step at a time. Yes, to the faint of heart each of the first ninety-nine of those steps represents a failure of sorts. But to those with the determination to stay the course, success is inevitable.

Sincerely,

Harvey Mackay

*"You can't be brave
if you've only had
wonderful things
happen to you."*

Mary Tyler Moore

BRENDAN R. BANAHAN
PUBLISHER

...is the publisher of FIELD & STREAM and OUTDOOR LIFE, the nation's two largest outdoor magazines.

Brendan describes in his letter the most common reaction he receives upon being introduced to someone new. When we met several years ago, it was my reaction, too. I could not believe that someone so young was the top guy at not one, but two major magazines.

Before taking responsibility for two of Times Mirror's largest publications, Brendan spent almost a decade with Time Incorporated where he most recently served as advertising director for MARTHA STEWART LIVING. Prior to that, he was the New York advertising director for PEOPLE MAGAZINE.

As I have gotten to know Brendan, I have come to admire him and his abilities. I have also heard stories about his "problem" of not being the proper age! When there were those who would deny him the experience needed to advance, Brendan found opportunity in other places.

FIELD&STREAM

OUTDOORLIFE

Brendan R. Banahan
Publisher

Mr. Andy Andrews
P.O. Box 2761
Gulf Shores, Alabama 36547

Dear Andy:

It is a rather onerous task to represent the accumulated knowledge of the outdoors embodied in the titles of *Field & Stream* and *Outdoor Life*. I have been given a tremendous responsibility at an early age to manage two of America's most respected outdoor magazines. In fact, I have often been introduced to individuals or groups only to have someone stop me at some point and say, "We expected you to be older." Age is not a function of ability or desire to be the best at what you do.

While this may be disarming for some, it can present a problem for others. I have been the "youngest" staff member or manager in a number of situations in the past. While I have been known to be rather strong-willed and maybe even opinionated, I have worked hard to earn the respect of those individuals who would be an obstacle to the success of a project or your entire business. I believe in listening, asking questions and seeking the advice of respected experts on subjects of personal and professional importance. No matter how much you think you know about a subject or how skilled you become, there is always someone more proficient than you. Find them!

My parents always encouraged excellence. Choose a career they said, grand or obscure, but be the best in your field. I encourage all outdoorsmen to be the best representatives of our sports. Respect the environment, observe all game laws and prove to those individuals that oppose our rights that not all of us will exploit all species to extinction.

I have been very fortunate to combine my passion for the outdoors with a career in this exciting, wonderful industry. It has brought me into contact with exceptionally thoughtful individuals like you. My best wishes for continued success and many safe hunting and fishing seasons to come.

Best regards,

Brendan R. Banahan
■ Times Mirror
■ Magazines
Two Park Avenue
New York, NY 10016
(212) 779-5230

SHIRLEY JONES
ENTERTAINER

...is an Academy Award winner who has starred in countless major motion pictures and Broadway plays. She has maintained star status for more than four decades.

In 1952, after being named Pittsburg's Crown Princess, Shirley Jones borrowed $160 from her father and headed to New York. She promised to return after the money was gone, but that was never to be. Her Broadway career began with a role in "South Pacific".

Then came Hollywood. After being named the female lead in the movie "Oklahoma", she was soon America's sweetheart. The movie follow-ups to "Oklahoma" came fast and furious for the nation's new girl next door: "The Courtship of Eddie's Father" and "Ticklish Affair" with Glenn Ford; "The Cheyenne Social Club" with Jimmy Stewart and Henry Fonda; and of course the classic "Carousel".

Shirley captivated audiences for over four years with her role as "Marion" in the Broadway hit "The Music Man", then starred in the motion picture with Robert Preston. She also won an Oscar for "Elmer Gantry".

I'll always remember Shirley as the mother of the "Partridge Family" and as Marion the librarian in "The Music Man". The show was a favorite of mine growing up and the movie is a favorite still!

Dear Andy,

When I was first asked to contribute here by describing the most memorable "obstacle" or "setback" in my life, I was sure I'd have to decline. For ME, in MY memory, there weren't any. Both my personal and professional lives have always gone letter perfect, at least the way I saw it.

But, strange as it may seem, those closest around me have a different view. They all, to the very last one, share the common belief that "Shirley Jones is her OWN obstacle"; that, were it not for my own "lack of singular drive and ambition," my career would be considerably more active and more substantial. They cite, with great bewilderment, the super opportunity time-period immediately after receiving my Academy Award in 1961 (Elmer Gantry-Best Supporting) as the year I decided to drop out and have my first baby, thereby losing the flood of academy-calibre role offers that invariably pour in right after an Oscar win (and sometimes never again). And so, the way they see it, I AM my own obstacle.

The fact is, they're right. The great fame and adulation "rewards" that fire destined careers to dizzying heights never sparked a flicker for me. I don't know exactly why, but I never needed it, never wanted it, never understood it. The simpler rewards of personal achievement - my voice and my music - came early, but were quickly engulfed by the Hollywood Hustle Machine, the army of agent-manager-press agent warriors that move in to "groom" you and "package" you and "market" you like some new pink detergent in town with a shot to beat out the others and take all the marbles. For some, the added hassle of that day-to-day chase is exciting and positive. For me, it's alien and offensive, all of it.

And there's no "happy ending" to this obstacle story. It's a struggle I still deal with almost every day. Were it mine to choose, I'd give it all up and retire to my glorious Big Bear mountain retreat. But, I guess my husband and the rest of the business team's got me convinced my public message isn't "through" yet - that delivering it in full is as much an OBLIGATION to God's gift as it is a REWARD for it.

And maybe they're right.

So, I'll hang on some more till it IS time to pack it in and surrender to what I've always felt to be my natural, chosen place..as far from all that big city jazz and pizzazz and me-too-mania as I can get.

Shirley Jones

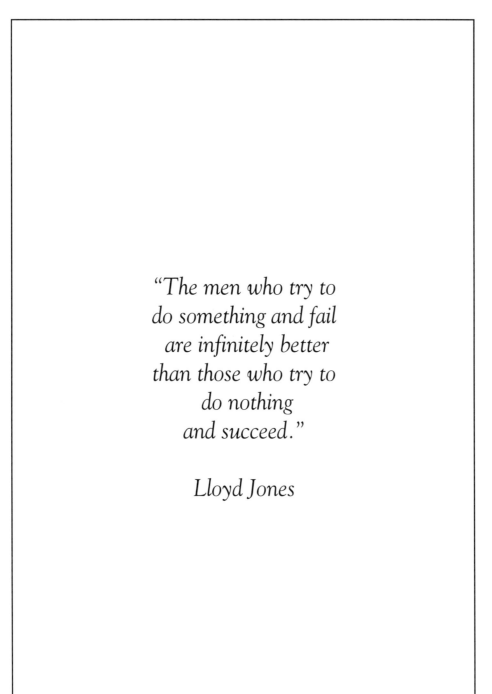

*"The men who try to
do something and fail
are infinitely better
than those who try to
do nothing
and succeed."*

Lloyd Jones

SUGAR RAY LEONARD
PROFESSIONAL BOXER

...held world titles in five different weight divisions. He appears regularly as a commentator for ESPN.

Sugar Ray Leonard has appeared at Caesars Palace more often than most entertainers...and the ticket price is always higher than that for a show. He is among the most recognizable athletes on the planet and yet, with all his success in boxing, Ray is now enduring another storm.

When I asked him to write a letter detailing a failure or rejection with which he had dealt, I assumed it would have something to do with starting his boxing career. I was pleasantly surprised, however, to see that he chose to write about a current challenge.

Many people assume that when one is visited by success, he or she has smooth sailing from that point. Just the opposite is often the case. Success creates it's own new challenges. Ray Leonard is a person who has learned that perseverance and preparation are the key to any victory, and presently, he is in another fight that he will win.

Ray C. Leonard
T/A Sugar Ray Leonard
4922 Fairmont Avenue, Suite 200
Bethesda, Maryland 20814
Tel. (301) 657-4771

Personal Secretary
Caren L. Kinder

Dear Andy,

To hear the word, rejection, creates a feeling of not being capable, not measuring up, a feeling of incompetence.

I can remember so vividly being rejected by the girls at the parties and the discos when I asked them so politely for a dance. It got so bad that I would become extremely shy, antisocial and introverted. I was able to get through those teenage years through boxing, a sport looked upon as inhuman, barbaric and outright inconceivable, but, to become the Champion of the World, and having a little marketable charm, all those girls that treated me like a pest were knocking at my door! Sorry, no one's home - Ha Ha! Now boxing is over and I want to go to Hollywood. I went to dozens of theatrical agencies, only to be patronized, talk shop and reflect on my illustrious boxing career! Great, but I wanted to work! - not become an overnight star, just get me work in one film. They kept their word and called me back, only to say, "Being Black is one thing, but being Black and a Boxer is twice as bad". Being Black, a former Boxer (and a famous one), was too much of a job, a risk, etc. "Good Luck, We Love Ya, Champ," they would say.

I had the pleasure of meeting Lou Pitt from ICM at a birthday party of a friend of my fiance. We had a brief talk - not much was said because it's not professional to discuss business at a private affair, but most importantly, I didn't want to be rejected, again. Weeks passed and I was asked to come in and meet with the staff of ICM so that they could get a feeling about me. I was asked to return again, and you know what?!! They represent me! This is not to say that I will become a major star, but to say that because of boxing I've always felt like No. 1 with confidence, pride and dignity, and ICM has taken a chance with me and I won't let them down!! Never let anyone deter you from your goal - no one!

All the best,

Sugar Ray Leonard

91

ALAN K. SIMPSON
UNITED STATES SENATOR

...is the author of the Immigration Reform and Control Act, the first major immigration reform legislation passed in over thirty years. He maintains a leadership role in the Senate as Assistant Republican Leader.

Alan Simpson was born September 2, 1931, and is a native of Cody, Wyoming. A member of a political family—his father served as both Governor and United States Senator from Wyoming—Al chose to follow in his father's footsteps and began his own political career in 1964. He served for the next thirteen years in the Wyoming House of Representatives holding the offices of Majority Whip, Majority Floor Leader and Speaker Pro-Tem.

In 1978, Al ran for, and was elected to, the United States Senate. After a successful first term, he was re-elected in 1984 with 78% of the vote and then again in 1990 to a third term.

Following his first term in the Senate, Al was elected by his peers to the position of the Assistant Majority Leader or "Majority Whip" in 1984. Since then, he has been re-elected to the position of Whip in each subsequent Congress, first in 1986 and then again in 1988 and 1990.

ALAN K. SIMPSON
WYOMING

United States Senate
WASHINGTON, DC 20510–5002

Andy Andrews
P.O. Box 2761
Gulf Shores, Alabama   36547

Dear Andy:

How goes things with you? I was pleased to receive your
recent letter and learn of your interest in including me in your
latest endeavor. I can surely tell you, Andy, that there have
been times in my life -- private, professional and political --
when I have felt the stinging pain of rejection, but let me
assure you that I always learned much more from the experience
than I could have ever imagined at the time!

One particular instance comes vividly to mind. I was a
freshman at the University of Wyoming Law School and I was not
doing too well -- that is a euphemism for "damn near flunking!"
I was studying in the evenings and on weekends with the same pals
who were getting A's in their courses and I was working as hard
as I could -- at least I thought I was! Yet, I must admit that I
was somewhat diverted. Not only was I going with a magnificent
woman (now my wife Ann) who was teaching grade school in
Cheyenne, Wyoming and traveling "over the hill from Laramie" to
see her often, but I knew that the Army was headed my way and I
would soon be shipped overseas. Looking back on it all it is
obvious I was not at the "peak of my game!"

I remember the trepidation I felt in being called to meet
with the Dean of the law school, one R.R. Robert Hamilton. He
sat me down and said, "Alan your work is not up to par. If things
do not come together I think you are going to have to consider
not going forward with a legal career. And yes, Al, I know your
father was a lawyer and your grandfather was a lawyer, but there
is no reason you should feel you should be 'locked into' that
same profession."

He went on in that vein and I finally said, "Look, Dean, I
have wanted to be a lawyer since I was five years old and I will.
I am going to get a law degree if I have to go to Panhandle A&M
to get it. Nobody is going to stop me!" He seemed quite
startled and he bridled a bit at my intensity. I was looking him

Andrews--Page Two

right square in the eye and I said, "I mean that. I'll get this degree. Damned if I care where." He admired that defensive vigor in me -- at least he reported it to me in a kindly way when we shared talk of the incident later in his life.

That was the first hurdle. I made it over after hooking my toe on it! Then in the second year of law school (after a two year break for Army service) I was researching and writing an article for the Law Review and the faculty advisor confided, "I have reviewed your work very carefully and I find a most remarkable thing. You have a very fine vocabulary and a way of writing with rather distinctive wit and humor. However, when you stray into uncharted waters and get into an area you do not understand well, you have this great propensity to cover it up with great obfuscation and ponderous verbiage." Boy that really smoked me! He went on slowly. "As soon as you learn to control that propensity to B.S. I know you will be doing a lot of good readable work and you will do very well in your last year of law school." I simply could not believe what I was hearing. Blood was rushing heatedly behind my eyeballs. I didn't know whether I wanted to pop the guy in the mush or just simply slink out of the place. But believe me when I say that I was listening intently to his every word. I eyed him carefully. I did notice that he was smiling and that he was not looking or being harsh. He was just so regrettably "on target."

I immediately went home to that former school teacher from Cheyenne. I said, "Let me tell you what this guy said." She understandingly said, "Tell me about it." I sure did. I even put my own spin and tilt on it and she said, in a level and thoughtful way, "But, Al, he might be right." And he was, and she was.

That got me started in life on a new learning curve and sorting process. It was a damn tough lesson for me to learn but a solid one. It helped me to grow up a bit more -- and I'm 6'7" so you know there was much physical growing already accomplished -- but not the other "kind" of growing! The main lesson was: Look 'em right in the eye -- and don't B.S. 'em. If you really don't know what the hell you are doing just tell them or pull in your horns and get out of the fray.

During the nearly thirty years of my life in politics I have taken -- and given -- some pretty good shots. Politics is not a game of beanbag -- it is a full contact sport! I have also embroiled myself in some real tangles with the media -- what one learns from that is quite simple -- but it was hard coming, "Never get in a fight with somebody who buys ink by the barrel -- because you will come out a loser." However, that doesn't mean that you should give up doing those things if you think you are right. I always remember something my dear old Dad said, "You gotta give as good as you get." He also taught me that an attack unanswered is an attack believed -- nay, even agreed to!

Pop was very right about another thing, too. He always said, "If you're damned if you do and damned if you don't -- then do!"

Andrews--Page Three

My grandfather's advice was handy too, Andy, it was, "I can't tell you how to succeed but I can sure as hell tell you how to fail -- and that's try to please everybody."

These are some of the glittering guideposts along my road in life. The great pleasure you bring to others reminds me what my dear mother shared, "Humor is the universal solvent against the abrasive elements of life." It is a great adventure and it will continue to be so -- I know I will just keep learning and growing until they throw me in the hole!

It is a great honor to be part of this delightful project. My best to you, Andy -- always.

With kind personal regards,

Sincerely,

Alan K. Simpson
United States Senator

AKS/tjw

RONNIE MILSAP
ENTERTAINER

...is one of country music's biggest superstars. He has won every major award the music industry has to offer.

Whenever I see Ronnie Milsap, I immediately notice his smile, which is a reflection of the music in his heart. Unlike many performers, Ronnie has the ability to take different musical styles and meld them into a sound that is all his own.

Perhaps more than any other entertainer before or since, Ronnie broadened country's base to include fans of all musical genre. He moved from R&B to country in 1973—the same year he was signed by RCA Records. The following year, he won his first Grammy.

He won additional Grammys in 1976 and 1981. In 1982, "Any Day Now" became Billboard's Song of the Year and in 1983, "Stranger In My House" won the Grammy. In 1985, the album "Lost In The Fifties" snared the overall Grammy Award for Best Album.

Ronnie has won Entertainer of the Year and Male Vocalist of the Year three different times and Album of the Year four times. He has been hailed as one of the most talented musicians of his generation and, because of his ability to persevere in times of trouble, he is also one of the most inspiring.

12 MUSIC CIRCLE SO. ● NASHVILLE, TENNESSEE 37203 ●

Mr. Andy Andrews
P.O. Box 2761
Gulf Shores, Alabama 36547

Dear Andy,

Congratulations on the wonderful success your STORMS OF PERFECTION VOLUME I has received; and thank you for asking me to be part of the continuing volumes.

If I may quote from my autobiography's forward..."I was born virtually blind and into poverty, abandoned by my mother, and placed in the custody of strangers by the age of six". That is the script that could have set the stage for the rest of my life, were it not for divine intervention, strict discipline, and my insatiable will power!

The most traumatic experience of all was perhaps the first one, when I, as a six year old, and having been raised by two loving grandparents in the mountains of North Carolina, was taken to the Governor Morehead School for the Blind in Raleigh, and left to live and learn there for the next thirteen years. The Bible story I remembered best was the story of Joseph, who was sold into slavery as a youth. I was sure that I was a little boy who had been taken far away and sold into servitude. I didn't know which I felt more--heartbroken or betrayed! I cried bitterly for hours in a large hallway on a plastic mat! Being only six years old and left at that unfamiliar school that day was my closet brush ever with self-pity. But, through the incredible instruction and extreme discipline at that school, I would soon learn to abandon forever feeling sorry for myself.

The formation of will power wasn't entirely voluntary. I have it because at times I had nothing else. Quitting has never been an option. I think anybody can do virtually anything if he or she wants to badly enough. It's almost a blessing that I was born blind. I was ultimately taken out of the environment that my father's family and all the generations before me had been in.

(1)

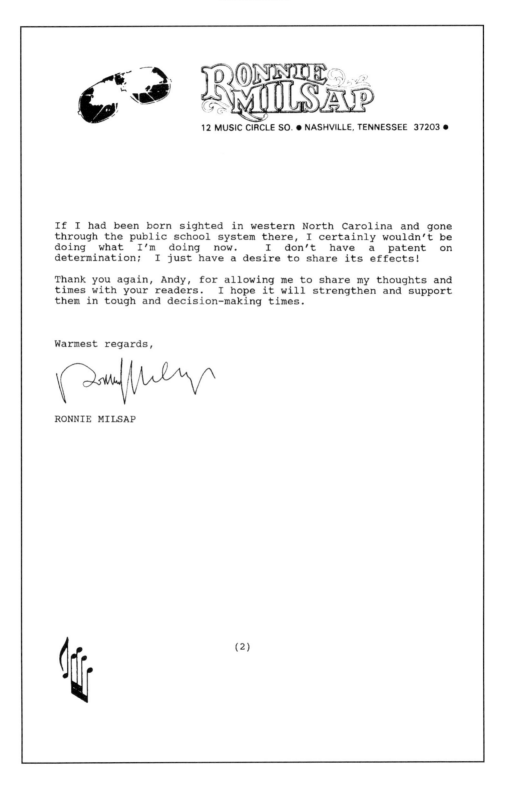

RONNIE MILSAP

12 MUSIC CIRCLE SO. ● NASHVILLE, TENNESSEE 37203 ●

If I had been born sighted in western North Carolina and gone through the public school system there, I certainly wouldn't be doing what I'm doing now. I don't have a patent on determination; I just have a desire to share its effects!

Thank you again, Andy, for allowing me to share my thoughts and times with your readers. I hope it will strengthen and support them in tough and decision-making times.

Warmest regards,

RONNIE MILSAP

(2)

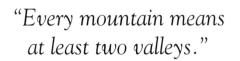

*"Every mountain means
at least two valleys."*

Anonymous

JOHN SCHUERHOLZ
GENERAL MANAGER
ATLANTA BRAVES

...was formerly General Manager of the Kansas City Royals. He has twice been named Major League Baseball's Executive of the Year.

I was excited when John Schuerholz agreed to provide a letter for this collection. We were quail hunting in Albany, Georgia with the folks from Quail Unlimited when I heard his story.

Many people have tunnel vision when dealing with what they want out of life. John was diverted from his initial goals and dreams, but went on to be a part of the game he loved. He has also become an incredible success. After only four years with John as General Manager, the Royals won the World Series in 1985.

In 1990, John assumed the position of Executive Vice-President and General Manager of the Atlanta Braves. They had just finished that season mired in last place. Under John's leadership, the Braves went to the World Series the very next year. And the next! In fact, the Braves have won the National League West pennant every year since John arrived.

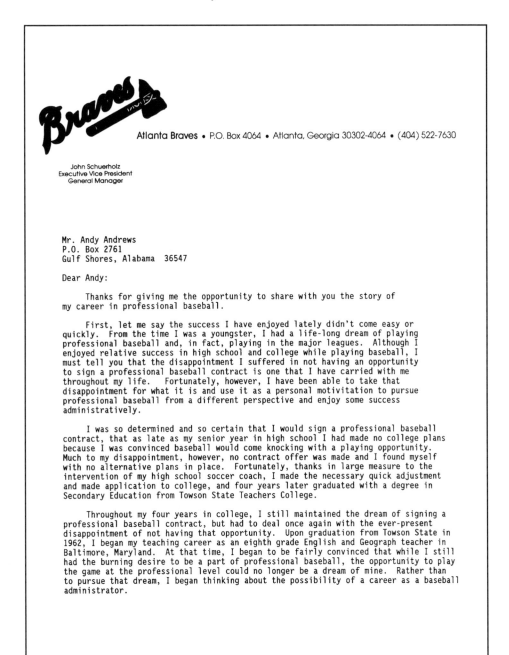

Atlanta Braves • P.O. Box 4064 • Atlanta, Georgia 30302-4064 • (404) 522-7630

John Schuerholz
Executive Vice President
General Manager

Mr. Andy Andrews
P.O. Box 2761
Gulf Shores, Alabama 36547

Dear Andy:

　　Thanks for giving me the opportunity to share with you the story of my career in professional baseball.

　　First, let me say the success I have enjoyed lately didn't come easy or quickly. From the time I was a youngster, I had a life-long dream of playing professional baseball and, in fact, playing in the major leagues. Although I enjoyed relative success in high school and college while playing baseball, I must tell you that the disappointment I suffered in not having an opportunity to sign a professional baseball contract is one that I have carried with me throughout my life. Fortunately, however, I have been able to take that disappointment for what it is and use it as a personal motivitation to pursue professional baseball from a different perspective and enjoy some success administratively.

　　I was so determined and so certain that I would sign a professional baseball contract, that as late as my senior year in high school I had made no college plans because I was convinced baseball would come knocking with a playing opportunity. Much to my disappointment, however, no contract offer was made and I found myself with no alternative plans in place. Fortunately, thanks in large measure to the intervention of my high school soccer coach, I made the necessary quick adjustment and made application to college, and four years later graduated with a degree in Secondary Education from Towson State Teachers College.

　　Throughout my four years in college, I still maintained the dream of signing a professional baseball contract, but had to deal once again with the ever-present disappointment of not having that opportunity. Upon graduation from Towson State in 1962, I began my teaching career as an eighth grade English and Geograph teacher in Baltimore, Maryland. At that time, I began to be fairly convinced that while I still had the burning desire to be a part of professional baseball, the opportunity to play the game at the professional level could no longer be a dream of mine. Rather than to pursue that dream, I began thinking about the possibility of a career as a baseball administrator.

Mr. Andy Andrews
Page 2......

Midway through my fifth year of teaching, I was about ready to complete my Masters Degree work in Supervision and Administration of Secondary Education. It was at that time that I decided to write a letter to the Baltimore Orioles applying for an administrative position with that organization. At this time, the good fortune of appropriate timing was on my side and I was invited to attend a job interview by the Orioles and, happily for me shortly thereafter, was offered an opportunity to begin a career as a baseball administrator with that organization.

I can't begin to share with you the depth of excitement and anticipation that I enjoyed at that time knowing that at last I would have an opportunity to be a part of professional baseball and would have the opportunity to begin a career in that profession. While I was at once delighted by this opportunity, the hard cold reality of the sacrifices of a new career became very apparent. to this day I believe that I am the only person to leave the teaching profession that had to take a reduction in salary to begin a career outside of the education field. I did that, however, when I joined the Baltimore Orioles simply to provide myself with the opportunity to experience a career in professional baseball.

Although my first desk in professional baseball was a portable typing table and my first real responsibility was filing and sorting various everyday documents, I knew almost from the very first day that this was where I was meant to be. My dream and my goal from that day forward was to become a Major League General Manager. I committed myself to that goal and dedicated myself to doing whatever was necessary to reach that goal. Happily, in October of 1981 at the age of 41, I was named General Manager of the Kansas City Royals and have enjoyed having the opportunity to continue as a General Manager to this day.

As you now know, I am in my third year as General Manager of the Atlanta Braves and while my first two years with this organization have provided as much excitement and enjoyment as any years in my baseball life, I often think back to how my career as a baseball administrator really began because of the rejection I experienced as a hopeful player. While I still wonder about the judgment of the scouts who overlooked my playing ability, I am thankful that that specific rejection proved to be a springboard for the success and enjoyment I have had these past 27 years.

Sincerely yours,

John Schuerholz
Executive Vice President
and General Manager

JS/jc

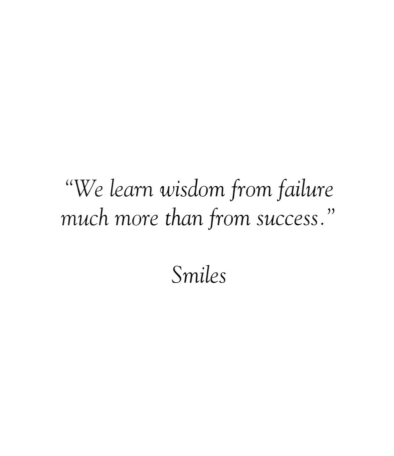

"*We learn wisdom from failure much more than from success.*"

Smiles

DR. JOYCE BROTHERS
PSYCHOLOGIST

...has been the world's most popular psychologist for more than three decades.

Dr. Joyce Brothers is not only the most popular psychologist in the world; she is easily the most recognized. She is known to millions as "The Mother of Media Psychology".

A best-selling author and columnist for Good Housekeeping, Dr. Brothers offers sound, professional advice six days a week to readers of more than 175 newspapers coast to coast. These include the <u>New York Daily News</u> and the <u>Los Angeles Times</u>. Her advice hotline is featured in <u>USA Today</u>'s "Lifeline" section.

She is heard daily on the NBC Radio Network and appears periodically on Fox Network's "A Current Affair" and KCBS in Los Angeles. In addition to this heavy schedule, she does frequent spots for other network shows. Dr. Brothers has made more guest appearances on television talk shows than any other non-performer in history.

JOYCE D. BROTHERS, PH. D.

1530 PALISADE AVE.

FT. LEE, N. J. 07024

(212) 831-2221

Mr. Andy Andrews
P.O. Box 2761
Guld Shores, Al 36547

Dear Andy:

When you asked me to write a letter concerning a
"Storm" in my life, I certainly didn't have to
search my memory to find one! I believe that any
truly successful person has suffered more than the
average amount of rejection in their life. Often,
these rejections are focused on one's ideas, abilities, or even appearances. In my case, however, the
most troubling rejection I experienced early in my
career, happened as a result of my gender.

In the early fifties, I was accepted into the Masters
and Doctoral program at Columbia University. This was
a very high honor. Columbia was, and remains, one of
the top Universities in my field in the country.

Soon after being accepted, the head of the department
sent word that he wanted to meet with me. This was a
very exciting prospect for I assumed he intended the
time as a greeting. After all, I had posted high marks
as an undergraduate entering the program.

As I walked into his office, I knew immediately that
he was not chairing the Welcome Committee. In fact, he
suggested I go elsewhere--find another school. I
would, he explained, take the place of a man who could
better make use of the education.

Believe it or not, at the time, I actually thought I
was in the wrong--that I had done something to merit
this treatment. But, realizing that Columbia had the
best training available, I calmly told him, "I will
stay".

"We'll make it tough", he assured me. And they did--
right up until the time I finished. During my orals, I
was pregnant. The Professor kept me on my feet answering
questions for six hours.

Looking back, I am thankful we have come a long way,
but I am also thankful for some of my early struggles.
Those struggles in my life have played a major role in
the success I have experienced. The struggles, you see,
made me strong.

Stand your ground. It will be worth it!

Sincerely,

Joyce D. Brothers, Ph.D.

MARTY INGELS
ENTERTAINER/ ENTREPRENEUR

...is a former comedian and actor. He is now the largest packager of celebrity promotional and endorsement campaigns in the world.

With all attempts at a "normal" job dead-ending early, Marty Ingels embarked on a show business career in 1957. Tenacious and talented, he rode the comedy rails to national prominence as the raspy voiced star of the ABC series "I'm Dickens, He's Fenster".

As Marty reveals in his incredible letter, all that he had worked for came to a crushing end in a most humiliating, public way. He did, however, emerge from his storm a stronger, more determined person.

Marty Ingels now owns and operates the "Celebrity Brokerage" with offices in New York, Chicago, Dallas, London, and Tokyo. He is the largest and most successful packager of celebrity endorsements in the world.

With all his accomplishments, Marty is perhaps best known for his wacky, whimsical courtship of (and subsequent marriage to) Shirley Jones. A book about that time in their lives, "Marty and Shirley, An Unlikely Love Story" was a best-seller in 1991 and is soon to be a TV movie.

Okay, Andy, you asked for it !

My story's not gonna be like the others. But I know that this "obstacle" tale will hit home for so many people out there who think, as I did during my terrible time, that they are all alone.

Most of us would perceive an "obstacle" story to concern some sort of Snag or Stumbling-Block on the road to success. But how about a situation where <u>SUCCESS ITSELF</u> was the Snag and the Stumbling-Block?? - And, when you think of it, aren't there many people you know who are as AFRAID and INTIMIDATED by the very **"achievement"** they claim to seek, as they are driven and dedicated to it ??? For me, it was a constant ambivalent agony. In my head there were **two** loud and unceasing voices, one pushing me on every minute of every day to uncompromising victory everywhere, assuring me always of my capability and my worth; And the other, mocking, deriding, and sabotaging all of it at every turn, undermining and decrying each step forward with a thousand frightful reasons to fall back and lose.

And I <u>SEEMED</u> to be beating it. My "Good Guy" voices <u>SEEMED</u> to be drowning out the other ones. It was 1964. I was young and healthy, in Hollywood less than a year, and already the star of my own network TV sitcom ("I'm Dickens, He's Fenster" - ABC). But, alas, those creeping sounds of doom and defect were not to surrender without a last counterattack. They were about to mount their dark dismal launches and hit the beach with everything they had.

It began as little "nerve" sieges - rashes, nausea, shortness of breath. Then worse - headaches, chest pain, dizziness, and panic so acute it was hard to carry on. And little by little I carried on less and less, dreading normal encounters, the simplest responsibilities, even the hard-won audience exposures I had thrived on for so long.

That next week I was to appear on "The Tonight Show" with Johnny Carson (a super pinnacle in my business) and there, sitting on that famous couch and before the entire world, my whole professional life would come to a mystifying and cataclysmic end in the virtual flash of an instant.

Carrying on one of my routine stories, I suddenly felt a kind of "trembling" in my toes and my right leg. I tried to ignore it and continue, but it slowly began traveling to my knee and my thigh and then my whole right side, which was now beginning to lose its feeling. I had anxiety attacks before, but this one was different. It was unyielding and horrendous and it wasn't going away. By now my whole body was numb, and tingling like a zillion little needles. It was like I was just "slipping away" little by little, right there on network television. And the more I fought it, the more I twisted and turned in that chair, trying to sit on my hands and rattle my feet, the louder the audience laughed. Crazy Marty was at it again. What a card !

Suddenly my hearing started to dim, my head got lighter, and (I think we've all had that terrifying feeling) "pieces of the vision puzzle" started falling away. All I could think of was getting off that stage before I lost consciousness. True comic to the last, I mustered the strength to stand up and announce that I would be the first guest to ever use Johnny Carson's private bathroom, and off to the rear I staggered, the audience still howling, and Johnny himself plainly dumbfounded. I managed to make it to the curtain, which I held tightly onto, swinging myself around to the other side, where I just dropped into the waiting arms of the backstage crew. They carried me to my dressing room, and then to my car and to my Hollywood apartment. Inside, they bundled me up in a big woolen blanket that was lying on my living room floor in front of the TV (ironically, a familiar place of refuge during past anxiety attacks) and left me there, conscious, terrorfied, and waiting for the only sure deliverance, sleep. As always, whatever this oneboggling seizure was, it'd be gone in the morning. This time I was wrong.

Incredibly, I lay on that floor, on that very spot in that dingy apartment building, for nine months, three weeks, and four days, crawling to the kitchen, crawling to the bathroom, and back to my little fetal nest on the floor. There was no family and few Hollywood friends to see me through this nightmare even I couldn't understand. Were it not for a young and obese neighbor next door (herself a kidney-transplant home-dialysis shut-in) who brought me hot food for all those months, I would truly have expired there on that dismal apartment floor.

There are lots of theories about what it was that hit me so hard and almost counted me out, from "complete clinical depression" to Hypoglycemia and all the fancy nouveau diagnoses in between. What is more important is that, whatever it was that KO'd me for all those long and agonizing months, found it timely to just disappear...all at once..one Sunday afternoon, just like that, and bring me back to life again..older, wiser, stronger for what I'd survived, and determined to keep the list of fervent promises I had made to myself while I was down there, bent and beaten. They spoke of not making any of the mistakes I'd made before, of having the strength to hold tight to the dream and the purpose and to all the pure objectives no matter what; And, most of all, of never being "scared" again - for what, NOW, was there to be scared OF ? I had already been beyond the gates of Hell and there were no other places left but UP.

(I spend a good deal of time now telling my story to groups of all sizes at schools and seminars and rehab centers across the country. Somehow, it makes its point and serves its purpose by the mere telling. Most of the people in those seats are only too familiar with the early thoughts and feelings that pushed my final crash, and, from what they've come to tell me, tapping into them and sharing them has worked wonders, perhaps even sparing them the likes of the holy nightmare that was mine.)

Marty Ingels

VINCENT J. DOOLEY
ATHLETIC DIRECTOR
UNIVERSITY OF GEORGIA

...was formerly the Head Football Coach at the University of Georgia where he won a National Championship and six SEC Championships.

It is difficult for me to imagine Vince Dooley as a football coach, yet he is one of the most successful in history. When he retired, he ranked third nationally in total victories among active coaches. It is tough to imagine Vince as a coach because he is, well...nice.

He is polite. I laughed when he introduced himself to my wife. "Hi, I'm Vince Dooley." It may seem like a little thing, but many people of his stature never say their name when they meet someone. It is as if they assume we are supposed to know who they are. Vince is a nice, polite, humble man.

In the state of Georgia, he is so wildly popular that he has been urged to run for Governor. He never has, but he serves people in other ways. Easter Seals, Boy Scouts, the Heart Fund, and Juvenile Diabetes have all benefited from Vince Dooley's time. In 1987, he was actually named the National Volunteer of the Year for his service.

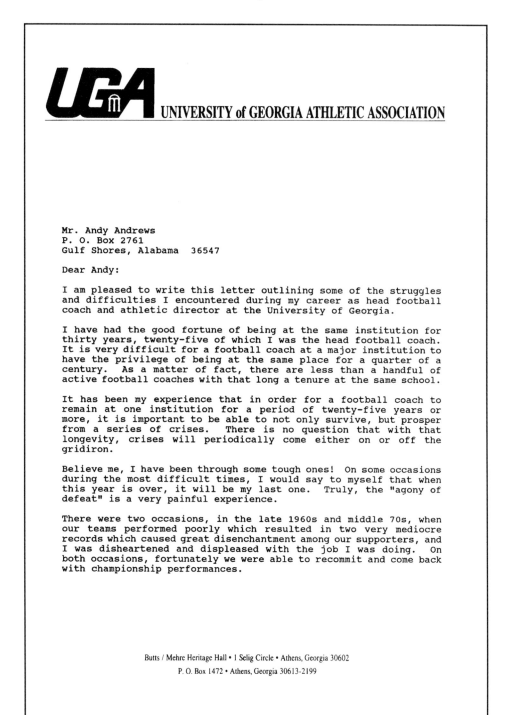

UNIVERSITY of GEORGIA ATHLETIC ASSOCIATION

Mr. Andy Andrews
P. O. Box 2761
Gulf Shores, Alabama 36547

Dear Andy:

I am pleased to write this letter outlining some of the struggles and difficulties I encountered during my career as head football coach and athletic director at the University of Georgia.

I have had the good fortune of being at the same institution for thirty years, twenty-five of which I was the head football coach. It is very difficult for a football coach at a major institution to have the privilege of being at the same place for a quarter of a century. As a matter of fact, there are less than a handful of active football coaches with that long a tenure at the same school.

It has been my experience that in order for a football coach to remain at one institution for a period of twenty-five years or more, it is important to be able to not only survive, but prosper from a series of crises. There is no question that with that longevity, crises will periodically come either on or off the gridiron.

Believe me, I have been through some tough ones! On some occasions during the most difficult times, I would say to myself that when this year is over, it will be my last one. Truly, the "agony of defeat" is a very painful experience.

There were two occasions, in the late 1960s and middle 70s, when our teams performed poorly which resulted in two very mediocre records which caused great disenchantment among our supporters, and I was disheartened and displeased with the job I was doing. On both occasions, fortunately we were able to recommit and come back with championship performances.

Butts / Mehre Heritage Hall • 1 Selig Circle • Athens, Georgia 30602
P. O. Box 1472 • Athens, Georgia 30613-2199

Page Two

Perhaps the worst year was in 1977, when I had my first and only losing season in my twenty-five years of coaching. Once again, however, there was a recommitment and a resolve that eventually led to not only a National Championship, but three Southeastern Conference Championships in a row and the best record in college football during a four-year period in the early 1980s.

Not only were there crises on the field that had to be addressed, but there were even more problems off the field. In the early '80s, we had a couple of bouts with the NCAA; although, I am proud to say that all of the problems were secondary and technical in that there was no pattern of violations. Yet, they were high profile media happenings that reflected poorly on the program.

Even more serious was the crisis known as the "Jan Kemp Incident." She was a former professor who won a lawsuit accusing the administration of firing her because of her objection to preferential treatment of athletes. The incident provoked an immediate media blitz for weeks and resulted in several investigations.

The University faculty formed an investigative committee. The Board of Regents of the University system investigated the allegations, as well as the State Attorney General's Office. During that time, there were many rumors and allegations, all of which were extremely discouraging at the time. In the final analysis, all of the investigations did not reveal any abuse on the part of the Athletic Department. There were mistakes made, but had the Athletic Department been guilty of some of the charges, there would have been no way that the program would have survived.

What really helped our program is when we realized there would be a continuation of daily allegations and unfounded charges, and concluded that if our program was strong and on a solid base, which we believed it was, then we would survive the strong winds of criticism. We took the attitude that while we cannot respond and answer every daily charge and criticism that appeared in the newspaper, we could use this crisis as an opportunity to make our program better.

When all of the investigations were over, we made some changes and addressed some of the problems. I am proud to say that in the final analysis, as a result of our attitude, our program was stronger than ever before. We had truly taken a crisis and turned it into an opportunity for a greater program. Despite this, it was extremely discouraging to have to go through that period of time.

Page Three

Andy, as you perhaps know, I enjoyed a very successful career here as a football coach, and I am proud to still be at the University of Georgia in directing the entire athletic program. As I look back on the twenty-five years, we truly had some struggling and difficult times, and I recall two quotes that I kept uppermost in my mind throughout my career. One was by the great Greek poet, Homer, who said, "Adversity excites talent that in more normal times lies dormant." And the German philosopher, Frederich Nietzche said, "That which does not destroy me strengthens me."

I believe that our talents were excited in those crises, and the fact that we were able to turn a crisis into an opportunity made us a much stronger program.

Kindest personal regards.

Sincerely,

Vincent J. Dooley
Director of Athletics

VJD/psb

SHARON WOOD
MOUNTAIN CLIMBER

...became the first North American woman to climb to the top of Mount Everest. She was also the first woman to be certified as a climbing guide by the internationally recognized Association of Canadian Mountain Guides.

When I read Sharon Wood's letter, I was struck by the extent to which she had turned her life around. Many people experience storms of their own creation and refuse to take responsibility for the aftermath. Sharon, as her letter reveals, made the decision to learn from her mistakes and take charge of her future.

Since Everest, Sharon has been climbing toward goals of a different sort—braving the podium as a public speaker. Recognizing that the challenges of a mountain parallel those of a striving individual, she shares the learning she most prizes from her experiences.

In terms of magnitude and fulfillment, Sharon is now meeting her greatest challenge as the mother of two young boys. Her favorite quote is Helen Keller's "Life is a daring adventure, or nothing at all." There seems to be little doubt that Sharon, her husband Chris, and their family will live out this philosophy.

One Step ▲ Beyond
WorldWide

Dear Andy,

In the preface of your first book you speak of your father's wise interpretation of the storm, how all things can be strengthened and renewed from enduring a storm. I too experienced a storm which left a lifetime impact on me.

I experienced a very short and stormy period in my teens. I was one of those kinds of kids parents hate to see their own kids hanging around with. I had struggled and failed to fit to other people's rules and standards. My reaction was disillusionment and rebellion, I did not believe I was responsible for what I did. I craved adventure and escape and found it in drugs and shoplifting.

My fifteenth summer culminated in two incidents, I had a very frightening experience with some bad drugs and I was caught shoplifting. These events left me feeling very shaken and ashamed at the same time. I vowed I would never feel that ashamed of myself again. I realized that no one could change what had happened and only one person could change the direction of my future.

It took this storm in my life to realize I was the writer, actor and director of my own play, the play being my life. This was a tremendously liberating notion that I had never considered before. I might be a misfit, but I was determined to find and cultivate an environment where I could not just fit and survive but thrive. This dissatisfaction provided me with the motivation to change the things that were not working for me.

I moved away from the overcrowded suburb I was living in to the mountains where my spirit soared. I left the educational system available to me and buried myself in books that educated me in the subjects I felt necessary to thrive as the person I could be. I searched out people with a similar love for the mountains and a quest for adventure and answers to the existential questions that plagued us all at that age.

I found a passion, a passion for climbing, something I could earnestly commit myself to, to struggle and endure. Climbing gave me an awareness of the huge gap between what I thought was possible and what really is possible. I became completely engrossed with the exploration of the potential of myself and others.

P.O. Box 990, Suite 200, 838 10th Street,
Canmore, Alberta, Canada T0L 0M0
Telephone: (403) 678-5255 Toll-free: 1-800-661-9400 Facsimile: (403) 678-4534

One Step ▲ Beyond
WorldWide

The storms, the environment, the people, the passion and the accomplishment of climbing the highest mountain in the world became the vehicle for me to re-enter the mainstream of life with a very different attitude. I now work as a successful motivational corporate speaker and continue to teach and guide in the mountains. I am also a mother of two young boys. My greatest accomplishment in life has been to transfer the lessons learned from my adventures in the mountains, storms and all, to the even greater adventure I live now, life.

Thank you for the opportunity to share this with you and your readers.

Sincerely yours,

Sharon Wood

"When you have to make a choice
and don't make it,
that is in itself a choice."

William James

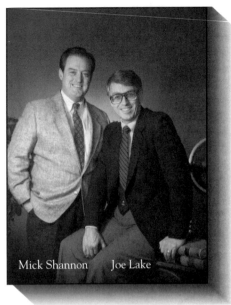

Mick Shannon   Joe Lake

JOSEPH G. LAKE
BUSINESSMAN

*…co-founded the CHILDREN'S MIR-
ACLE NETWORK and still produces
the annual telethon. Under his leadership, CMN has helped raise over a half
billion dollars for children's hospitals in
the United States and Canada.*

I first met Joe Lake at two o'clock in the morning. I was about to perform on the CMN telethon which was broadcast live from Disneyland. Joe
was moving through the crowd backstage, shaking hands and quietly giving
directions. I knew when I saw him that he was the guy about whom everyone had been talking.

I had heard all the stories—how he had worked for several years as the
advance man for the President. I knew he had been named Young
Businessman of the Year by the National Junior Chamber of Commerce
and that he had owned a large entertainment company dealing with live
events, record production, and management.

I also knew he had chucked it all for a dream. His dream was to create
funds and awareness for children's hospitals. And there was a twist. The
money raised in a local area would stay in that area. That is the way it is
still done today. Last year, Joe's dream raised 117 million dollars that went
directly to the hospitals. His letter describes the journey.

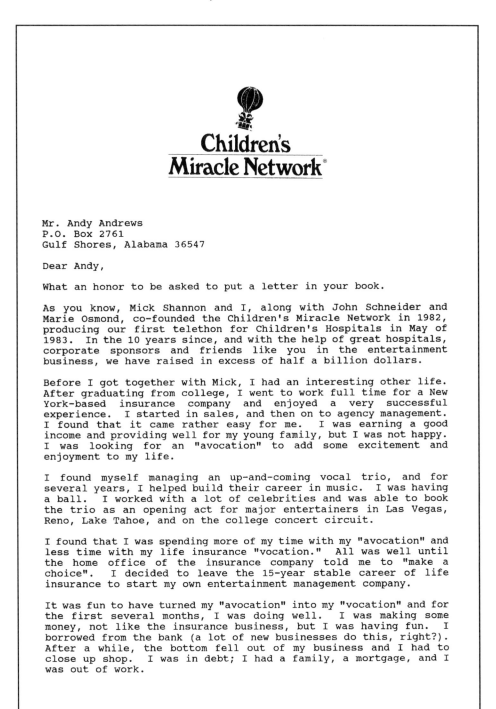

Children's
Miracle Network®

Mr. Andy Andrews
P.O. Box 2761
Gulf Shores, Alabama 36547

Dear Andy,

What an honor to be asked to put a letter in your book.

As you know, Mick Shannon and I, along with John Schneider and
Marie Osmond, co-founded the Children's Miracle Network in 1982,
producing our first telethon for Children's Hospitals in May of
1983. In the 10 years since, and with the help of great hospitals,
corporate sponsors and friends like you in the entertainment
business, we have raised in excess of half a billion dollars.

Before I got together with Mick, I had an interesting other life.
After graduating from college, I went to work full time for a New
York-based insurance company and enjoyed a very successful
experience. I started in sales, and then on to agency management.
I found that it came rather easy for me. I was earning a good
income and providing well for my young family, but I was not happy.
I was looking for an "avocation" to add some excitement and
enjoyment to my life.

I found myself managing an up-and-coming vocal trio, and for
several years, I helped build their career in music. I was having
a ball. I worked with a lot of celebrities and was able to book
the trio as an opening act for major entertainers in Las Vegas,
Reno, Lake Tahoe, and on the college concert circuit.

I found that I was spending more of my time with my "avocation" and
less time with my life insurance "vocation." All was well until
the home office of the insurance company told me to "make a
choice". I decided to leave the 15-year stable career of life
insurance to start my own entertainment management company.

It was fun to have turned my "avocation" into my "vocation" and for
the first several months, I was doing well. I was making some
money, not like the insurance business, but I was having fun. I
borrowed from the bank (a lot of new businesses do this, right?).
After a while, the bottom fell out of my business and I had to
close up shop. I was in debt; I had a family, a mortgage, and I
was out of work.

4525 SOUTH 2300 EAST • SUITE 202 • SALT LAKE CITY, UTAH 84117 • 801-278-8900 • FAX 801-277-8787

THE OSMOND FOUNDATION

I spent 8 months trying to find a full time career opportunity that I could enjoy and still feed my family. Nothing came my way. I was an out-of-work, over-qualified college graduate.

I had been a volunteer for a charity in Salt Lake City that did an annual "local" telethon. I recruited the celebrities for this annual event. The executive director of the charity was Mick Shannon. He and I became friends working a few weeks a year together on the local telethon.

During my "out of work period", Mick called and asked me if I would be willing to work for two months to prepare for the local telethon and I said yes. Fortunately, at the end of the two months, he asked me to stay, and together, we worked on an idea he had to take our "local" telethon to "national" status.

We worked together for three years with this charity to expand the telethon into more cities. I was working hard to recover from the failure of my business. I had lost my home and had to rent a small house, but I was working and I was happy. It was not easy. I had to travel a lot, but I was doing something that I felt was important.

After three years, the charity we were working for decided that they did not want to go "national" with our idea, and so we did an unbelievable thing. We both quit! Everyone thought I was off my rocker to give up a pay check after what I had been through. But Mick's idea of a national telethon was a great idea. I believed in Mick, and together we believed in the idea of doing a national telethon for kids. Because of our relationships with John Schneider and Marie Osmond, we all joined forces, and in 1982 co-founded the Osmond Foundation/Children's Miracle Network.

We are now into our 11th year and expect to raise in excess of $110 million this year for our 165 hospitals for children!

If I had never left the security of the insurance business and if I had never started a business that failed, I never would have been in the position to become partners with Mick Shannon in starting Children's Miracle Network. I hated the 8 months I looked for work. I hated the feelings of not being worth anything. I felt I was a failure. But I never gave up. I worked hard and started over and my family was at my side through it all.

I cannot thank Mick Shannon enough for having confidence in me, allowing me to share in his dream, and inviting me to become his partner.

If you believe in yourself and believe in others, you cannot fail. I am proud of the dream Mick and I, along with so many others, have built, but I appreciate most of all, the belief Mick had in me that allowed me to believe in myself again. We are doing good things for the children of the world, and as Moses Maimonides said, "If I am not for me, who will be for me? But, if I am only for me....what am I?"

Because I failed at one business, another opportunity, a much more satisfying one, became a reality. Never give up, never doubt yourself and what you can do...with help from good friends.

Kindest Personal regards,

Joseph G. Lake
Co-Founder
Executive Vice President and C.O.O.
Executive producer, Children's Miracle Network Telethon

LUIS COSTA
ENTREPRENEUR

…was born in Havana, Cuba on August 24, 1960. In January of 1982, he escaped to start a new life. He is now one of the wealthiest men in Spain.

Many people stare at opportunity every day of their lives and never do anything about it. For whatever reason they are too busy, too tired, too poor, too lazy, or too scared. Most of us will never know the dilemma into which Luis Costa was born. Communism presents no opportunity.

Luis dreamed of a day when he could live as he pleased. He wanted to provide a type of security for his family that was virtually unknown in Cuba. By sheer force of will and his ability to focus on a single-minded goal, Luis gained his freedom at the age of 21. This is his story.

Luis now lives in Madrid with his wife Christina and their children. He is the owner of an editorial agency, a travel agency, a production company, two accounting offices, and an international Amway distributorship with operations all over Europe, Mexico, Brazil, Argentina, and the United States.

 , S.L.

Antonio Cavero, 43 C
Tels.: (91) 388 40 69 / 388 49 62
Fax   (91) 759 85 16
28043 Madrid - España

Dear Andy,

    As you already know I was born in Cuba, and being a
comunist country as it is there was no opportunity or room
for free enterprise. At the age of 15, I realized that if I
were to acheive my dreams I had to leave Cuba, but the
question was, how?

    I was a good student and when I finished High School I
could opt for a University scholarship in a any one of the
Eastern Europeon countries and take advantage of the
opportunity to escape to the west. This was the beginning of
my plan of action.

    In order to receive the scholarship, good grades were
not the only thing that was needed, you also had to have a
good political report. So, at the age of 16, I joined the
Union of Young Comunists (youth organization which is the
"farm" for future members of the Comunist Party), I went to
all the youth and mass demonstrations organized by Castro's
regime. During summer vacations, instead of enjoying the
beach I would go to the work farms to cut sugar cane. All of
this gave me extra points and when I finished High School, at
the age of 18, I was given a Scholarship to study in Poland.
The first step was taken.

    I arrived in Poland in the summer of 1979 at the same
time the Polish people, led by Lech Walesa (today the
President of Poland) the leader of the famous Solidarity
Workers Union, were rebelling and I found myself in an
environment which confirmed my idea that there was no sense
for such a system.

    During the summer of 1981, along with a Peruvian freind
of mine whom was helping me, I tried to pass over to West
Berlin. In order to do this we went to the German and U.S.
embassies in Warsaw and U.S. consulate in Cracow. They all
told me they could not give me a visa since I was Cuban.
After this my freind Anita went to West Berlin to try and get
me a false passport.

    While she was in Berlin, on December 13, 1981, there was
a coup d etat by General Jaruselski and the entry into Poland
of all foreigners was prohibited. At that same time, the
Cuban government, seeing what was going on started to get
uneasy thinking that their students might be influenced by
what they were seeing and also fight for their freedom and
decided to send all of their students to continue their
studies in Russia.

I was totally against this since I knew that the return trip of all the Cuban students in Russia was by boat from the port of Odessa and I would not be able to put into action the second part of my plan.

I asked to return to Cuba and finish my studies in Havana and was authorized to do so by the Cuban government. My return ticket was from Prague, Checoslovacia and I knew that the plane had to do a tecnical layover in a western airport. I had heard stories of Cubans who had escaped either in Spain or Canada when the plane stopped n a layover.

So then I redesigned my plan of action. A few days before leaving Warsaw to Prague (I had a ticket for Prague - Havana for the 1/31/82) I talked to a Cuban sailer who told me that sometimes that flight went directly to Cuba with no stops.

The day of the flight, I was mentally prepared to break a leg or accidentally fall down a flight of stairs so I would miss that flight and get on the next one a week later. Thankfully, I did not need to do any of that since my flight would be stopping over in Madrid, Spain. Once someone asked me what would have happened if the flight would have been the direct flight. Andy, thank God, I did not have to go through that obstacle to reach my goal.

This is how on January 31, 1982 at 20:00 I declared myself a free man. Immediately, I realized that I was only politically free and thus another battle begun and that one was for my economic freedom.

Andy, I arrived in Madrid on a Sunday afternoon and there were no social institutions open so I spent my first night in the west in jail.

The following day, Feb. 1, 1982, I went to the Red Cross and Maruxa de la Rocha (now a very good friend of mine) helped me out. When I mentioned that I had spent my first night of freedom in jail, she said, "Luis, the important thing is not where you start but how you end up." I smiled and said, "Maruxa, in ten years I will be financially free.

Nine years afterwards, in April of 1991, after a lot of obstacles, I reached the level of Diamond in my Networking business and I had achieved financial freedom.

Today, I continue to live in Madrid. I am married and have two children, Keith, 4 1/2 and Kimberly, 2 1/2 and my wife, Cris is expecting our third child any day now. We would like to have six children. Number three is a boy and his name will be Kevin.

Our financial freedom today means we can make our decisions without having to consider the money or time involved. We are able to travel to places such as Hawaii, the Caribean, Florida, Mexico, Argentina and all over Europe. We are able to drive luxurius Mercedes and BMW's. Right now we are building an 1800 m2 house on the mediterainean.

Andy, dreams do come true if you are able to see the obstacles as opportunities to grow and become the person God intended you to be when he created you.

Thank you for the opportunity and honor to be part of this book and share it with so many people that I appreciate and admire.

My best regards,

Luis Costa

DALE EARNHARDT
RACE CAR DRIVER

...is a five-time NASCAR Winston Cup Series Champion. He is the three-time NMPA Driver of the Year.

The 1991 Winston Cup season produced a fifth series championship for GM Goodwrench Chevrolet driver Dale Earnhardt and the fourth for Richard Childress racing. All of RCR's titles have come in the last six years with Dale as the driver.

He took over the points lead in May and held it for the remainder of the season. Dale won four regular events en route to the title as well as the season opening Busch Clash. He also won the Daytona 500 qualifying race. That championship year produced earnings of $2,396,685—the highest in NASCAR history.

Dale Earnhardt has many career milestones. In 1987 and 1990, he was the winner of The Winston which made him the event's only two-time winner. Dale is also the only four-time winner of the Busch Clash and was 1979's Winston Cup Rookie of the Year.

Goodwrench

Racing

Andy Andrews
P.O. Box 2761
Gulf Shores, AL 36547

Andy,

When I received your letter, I couldn't help but be interested in
the project. Too many times these days, when we reach a certain
level of success, there is a tendency to forget what got us there.
If that happens, there is a danger of losing touch with reality.
Because there are times when my life certainly doesn't seem real.

I was raised in the small mill town of Kannapolis, N.C. where hard
work was a way of life for everybody. But my father, Ralph, was not
a mill worker. He raced stock cars on the dirt tracks of the South
and was a champion. That left no question in my mind as to what I
wanted to be -- a racer and a champion.

I didn't finish my high school education against the wishes of my
dad and my mother, Martha, and I went to work. It's something I'm
strongly against today (I have two kids in college) but was
unfortunately common at that time. I did everything I could to make
a living for myself and my family and to make enough money to race.
I was running a local gas station when I was 16. I was the only one
who had a set of keys other than the owner and was the only one who
knew what to do when the place opened and when it closed. I would
open around six in the morning, work all day, go home and eat, take
a nap and come back and work until closing.

I had other jobs too. I worked as a welder and I mounted tires at
a local shop and on the weekends I raced. I went from Charlotte and
Concord, N.C., to Columbia and Spartanburg, S.C., to Georgia;
anywhere there was a race that I had time to get to. I hoped to
make enough during the week to pay the entry fee. If I didn't, I
would borrow and hope to win enough to pay back the loan on Monday.

I ran my first race on what is now the NASCAR Winston Cup circuit
in 1975 when Ed Negre put me in his car for the World 600. I ran
a race or two a year until William Cronkrite gave me the chance to
drive four races for him in 1978. Rod Osterlund then put me in his
car for one race and I finished fourth. He decided he would try to
run the full schedule in 1979 with me as driver.

Things began happening. I won my first Winston Cup race in only my
16th career start, won four poles in 1979 and was named the Rookie-
of-the-Year. The next season was even better. I won five races, had
19 top-five finishes and won the NASCAR Winston Cup championship.
I thought things were headed my way.

But, as often happens in racing, uncertainty became a problem. Osterlund sold the team and after a handful of races with the new owner, I decided to leave. I talked Richard Childress, who owned his own team, into letting me finish the season driving his car. Things went pretty well, but I didn't win a race and 1981 and remains the only year since 1978 I have not won. I mean, here I was the defending champion and I didn't have a full ride. It wasn't supposed to be this way.

At the end of the '81 season, I had a couple of opportunities to drive for other teams so I consulted Richard. He was just putting things together and said he thought I would have a better chance to win races and championships with another team. I left and had some limited success. Then after the 1983 season, Richard, who had remained my friend, and I were hunting and he said he was looking for another driver. He had built his organization much stronger than it was when I left and I had a sponsor so I re-signed with him for 1984. I have been with him since and we recently signed a contract extension through the 1996 season with each other and our sponsor, GM Goodwrench.

Along the way, I have won 53 races, five Winston Cup championships and have become the all-time money earnings leader in American Motorsports history. No more borrowing money on Friday and hoping I can win enough to pay it back Monday. I have had the support and encouragement of a lot of people, my wife Teresa, my children, Kerry, Kelley, Dale Jr., and Taylor and a lot of friends. Richard and the team have become the best in the business. I also have some of the greatest fans in the world. I have been blessed. I became a racer and have become a champion.

Satchel Paige once said "Don't look back, something might be gaining on you." I think, sometimes, you need to look back. Thanks, Andy, for reminding me to do so.

Sincerely,

Dale Earnhardt

*"The man who insists
upon seeing
with perfect clearness
before he decides –
never decides."*

Henri Frederic Amiel

TOXEY
HAAS
ENTREPRENEUR

*...took his love of hunting and the out-
doors and turned it into a multi-million
dollar camouflage enterprise.*

Toxey Haas is a likeable young man with an endless supply of enthusiasm. That trait obviously served him well as he encountered the obstacles
he describes in his letter.

I have spent a few of my favorite days in the woods and on the water
with Toxey and several of his associates. We weren't always successful in
our pursuit of game or fish, but as any outdoorsman knows, that is not the
purpose of the trip anyway. The enjoyment comes from other, more intan-
gible things. Toxey gets as excited about seeing a track as he does the real
deer and as excited about an early morning gobble as he does about the
actual turkey. This, he will tell you, is as it should be.

Toxey is a family man, a businessman, and a person to hold up as an
example of one who has his priorities straight. He is also a wonderful
example of a person who made something he loved into his life's work.

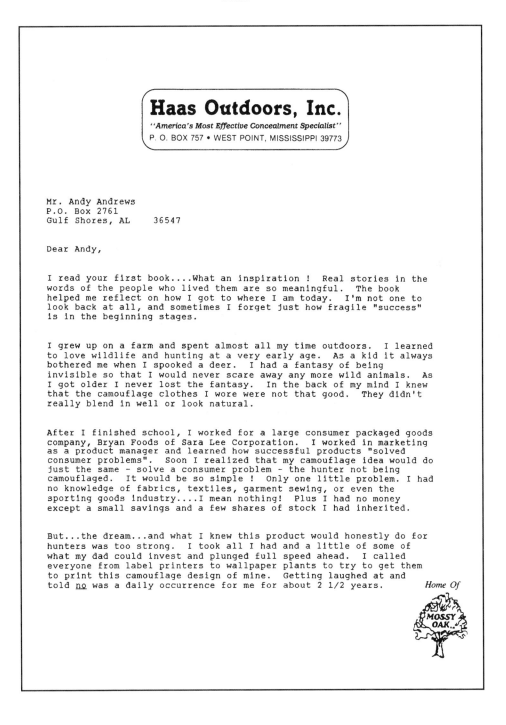

Haas Outdoors, Inc.

"America's Most Effective Concealment Specialist"

P. O. BOX 757 • WEST POINT, MISSISSIPPI 39773

Mr. Andy Andrews
P.O. Box 2761
Gulf Shores, AL   36547

Dear Andy,

I read your first book....What an inspiration ! Real stories in the
words of the people who lived them are so meaningful. The book
helped me reflect on how I got to where I am today. I'm not one to
look back at all, and sometimes I forget just how fragile "success"
is in the beginning stages.

I grew up on a farm and spent almost all my time outdoors. I learned
to love wildlife and hunting at a very early age. As a kid it always
bothered me when I spooked a deer. I had a fantasy of being
invisible so that I would never scare away any more wild animals. As
I got older I never lost the fantasy. In the back of my mind I knew
that the camouflage clothes I wore were not that good. They didn't
really blend in well or look natural.

After I finished school, I worked for a large consumer packaged goods
company, Bryan Foods of Sara Lee Corporation. I worked in marketing
as a product manager and learned how successful products "solved
consumer problems". Soon I realized that my camouflage idea would do
just the same - solve a consumer problem - the hunter not being
camouflaged. It would be so simple ! Only one little problem. I had
no knowledge of fabrics, textiles, garment sewing, or even the
sporting goods industry....I mean nothing! Plus I had no money
except a small savings and a few shares of stock I had inherited.

But...the dream...and what I knew this product would honestly do for
hunters was too strong. I took all I had and a little of some of
what my dad could invest and plunged full speed ahead. I called
everyone from label printers to wallpaper plants to try to get them
to print this camouflage design of mine. Getting laughed at and
told no was a daily occurrence for me for about 2 1/2 years.

Home Of

MOSSY
OAK..

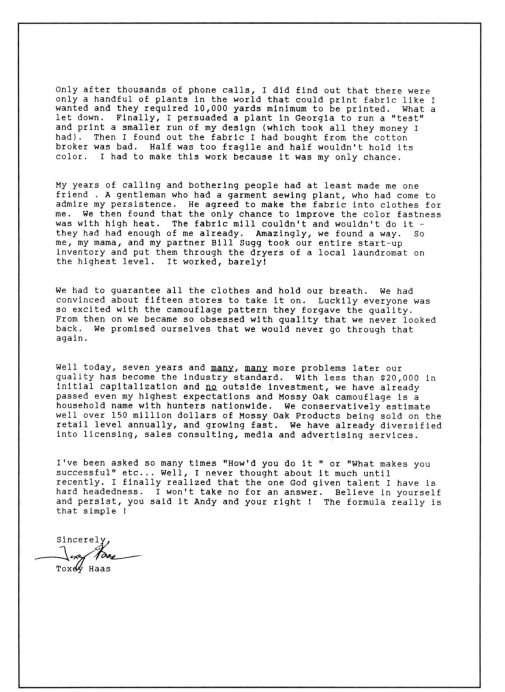

Only after thousands of phone calls, I did find out that there were
only a handful of plants in the world that could print fabric like I
wanted and they required 10,000 yards minimum to be printed. What a
let down. Finally, I persuaded a plant in Georgia to run a "test"
and print a smaller run of my design (which took all they money I
had). Then I found out the fabric I had bought from the cotton
broker was bad. Half was too fragile and half wouldn't hold its
color. I had to make this work because it was my only chance.

My years of calling and bothering people had at least made me one
friend . A gentleman who had a garment sewing plant, who had come to
admire my persistence. He agreed to make the fabric into clothes for
me. We then found that the only chance to improve the color fastness
was with high heat. The fabric mill couldn't and wouldn't do it -
they had had enough of me already. Amazingly, we found a way. So
me, my mama, and my partner Bill Sugg took our entire start-up
inventory and put them through the dryers of a local laundromat on
the highest level. It worked, barely!

We had to guarantee all the clothes and hold our breath. We had
convinced about fifteen stores to take it on. Luckily everyone was
so excited with the camouflage pattern they forgave the quality.
From then on we became so obsessed with quality that we never looked
back. We promised ourselves that we would never go through that
again.

Well today, seven years and <u>many, many</u> more problems later our
quality has become the industry standard. With less than $20,000 in
initial capitalization and <u>no</u> outside investment, we have already
passed even my highest expectations and Mossy Oak camouflage is a
household name with hunters nationwide. We conservatively estimate
well over 150 million dollars of Mossy Oak Products being sold on the
retail level annually, and growing fast. We have already diversified
into licensing, sales consulting, media and advertising services.

I've been asked so many times "How'd you do it " or "What makes you
successful" etc... Well, I never thought about it much until
recently. I finally realized that the one God given talent I have is
hard headedness. I won't take no for an answer. Believe in yourself
and persist, you said it Andy and your right ! The formula really is
that simple !

Sincerely,

Toxey Haas

*"Opportunity is missed by
most people
because it is dressed in overalls
and looks like work."*

Thomas Edison

MARY LOU RETTON
OLYMPIC GOLD MEDALIST

…was found to be the most popular athlete in America by a recent sports survey. In 1984, she became the first American woman ever to win a Gold medal in Gymnastics.

The more we saw Mary Lou in 1984, the more we loved her. She was (and still is) 4'9" tall and as she catapulted off the vault or whirled around the uneven bars we held our breath. When she landed, we jumped to our feet!

Mary Lou sprang into international fame by winning the All-Around Gold Medal in Women's Gymnastics at the 1984 Olympic Games in Los Angeles. She also won Silver medals for Team and Vault; and Bronze for Uneven Bars and Floor Exercise. Her five medals were the most won by any athlete at the '84 Olympics.

Mary Lou was once asked what she thought about before a competition. "I picture the victory," she said. "I see myself at the end of the event being awarded a perfect 10. I have the Gold medal around my neck. I picture the victory!"

MARY LOU RETTON

Mr. Andy Andrews
P.O. Box 2761
Gulf Shores, AL 36547

Dear Andy,

I'd like to share with you a story that not too many people are aware of. It was the Spring of 1984, the Olympic year. My right knee had been bothering me throughout my competitions that whole year. But as an athlete, you work with a little pain, so I didn't think much about it. But one night after an exhibition at a camp in Louisville, Kentucky, I knew something was really wrong.

So I walked up to my coach, Bela Karolyi and tapped him on the hip (Bela is 6'3", I'm 4'9"). With tears in my eyes, I said "Bela, I can't straighten my knee."

Bela told me to ice it and be back the next morning for workout. Well Bela isn't the kind of man you argue with, so I did as I was told. But the next morning the knee was swollen up like a balloon. They rushed me to the hospital, the doctor poked around and told me that I'd need surgery.

A piece of cartilage had broken off and gotten stuck in the knee joint. Even though it would be a relatively easy operation to remove it, I'd have less than six weeks to get back into Olympic shape. The doctors weren't very optimistic about my chances. They told me, no way. There wasn't enough time. One doctor even told me, "Go home and wait until the next Olympics."

I couldn't believe it. I had just come from winning the National Championships and the Olympic Trials. I was ranked #1 in American gymnastics. The dream that I'd had since I was 7 years old was going to come true: I was going to the Olympics! And now they were telling me to wait until the next Olympics. Well, nobody was going to tell ME what I could and couldn't do. Nobody was going to put limits on me.

So I had surgery right away, and I was barely out of recovery when they put me on a plane back to Houston. Two days later, I was back in the gym. Putting myself through one of the most difficult times in my life. Talk about frustration. A couple of days before, I had been in the best shape ever. And now, I was learning to walk all over again.

Well, I became a maniac. If they told me to do 20 leg-lifts, I'd do 100. I rode an exercise bike. I swam. I did everything on an apparatus that didn't involve tumbling or landing. And I did three months worth of rehabilitation in about three weeks. By the beginning of July, I was back to two-a-day workouts. When I got to Los Angeles, I was completely ready. And nobody but Bela and the doctors even knew I'd had surgery.

That's just one of the obstacles that I had to overcome in order to get to the Olympics. And believe me, every athlete who's achieved Olympic success has his or her own story of personal triumph. Because being the best means overcoming obstacles and giving that little bit extra. That's what separates the champions from the rest. That's true in sports, in business and in life.

Go for the Gold,

Mary Lou Retton

Mary Lou Retton

TIMOTHY D. VISLOCKY
STUDENT

...was one of the United States' most successful high school students in 1991. He is now enrolled at George Washington University in Washington, D.C.

Tim Vislocky was recognized by USA TODAY in 1991 as one of the most successful students ever produced by our country. Then, in June of that year, the bottom fell out. As he details in his letter, a near fatal boating accident caused a redirection of his goals.

Tim won first place in the Earth and Science category at the 1991 International Science and Engineering Fair. He was a National Merit Scholar and was actually awarded a research grant by the Atmospheric Science Field Laboratory.

Tim is also a musician. Having studied piano for 12 years, he won the National Piano Guild's International Award for Early and Advanced Bach. The greatest testimony to Tim's character, however, is his ability to rise above the storm life offered and continue to grow and achieve.

TIMOTHY D. VISLOCKY

1039 Cecil Place NW , Washington , DC 20007
(202) 338-4354

Andy Andrews
P.O. Box 71321
Nashville TN 37217

Dear Andy,

     The most significant setback in my life occurred rather recently. Actually, many people might consider everything in my life to be recent; I am only 20 years old. Anyway, in June of 1991, I was nearing the end of my final year in high school , with big plans for the future. As a high school junior, I was accepted by the University of Florida as an early admission student. This allowed me to participate in a program in which qualified rising high school seniors are allowed to enter the university after the completion of the eleventh grade. By entering college a year early, I could take much more challenging courses than those offered the high school during my "senior year" to give me an extra edge over my peers for the rest of my college years. I had just won the highest award possible in the physical sciences at the 1991 International Science and Engineering Fair: the first place Categorical Grand Award in Earth and Space Sciences. This was quite an honor, considering the competition which numbered several hundred, and included the best science students from high schools around the world. I won two congressional nominations to the U.S. Air Force Academy, and a four year full scholarship to any University of my choice, awarded by the Air Force. I was in excellent physical condition, with hopes of playing college football at either the Air Force Academy or some equally prestigious private school . In short, through the eleventh grade I enjoyed an extremely successful high school experience. Then, just one week before the end of school , The sky caved in on my little world.

     On June 1, 1991, I was severely injured in a boating accident while water-skiing with several friends. My right hip and upper leg were virtually torn apart by the boat's propeller. My injuries proved to be nearly fatal, and I was hospitalized for nearly four weeks, undergoing three surgical procedures to repair the bone, muscle, and nerve damage. At first, It was expected that I would lose my leg. Fortunately the primary surgeon treating me had some experience with a propeller injuries, and he was able skillfully prevent many potential complications, ultimately saving my leg.

While I was in the hospital, I had very little control over my condition. Narcotic pain killers which were prescribed to help combat the constant pain clouded my thinking and made it difficult to stay awake much of the time. Thanks to the excellent work of the team of doctors and nurses that treated me, I left the hospital with the chance to make a good recovery. It was at that point that I realized that my recovery was in my hands, not the doctors'. They saved my leg, but it was up to me to make it work again.

Initially I was confined to bed, with only occasional trips around the room in a reclining wheelchair. Any movement made me extremely weak, because I had not yet regenerated much of the blood I had lost during the accident. Gradually, I was able to stay out of bed longer every time I tried. Eventually, I began to use crutches to get around, and gradually started increasing the weight on my bad leg. I persisted, continually challenging my self with new and difficult physical feats, like walking to the window aided by just one crutch, or getting out of bed without any assistance. These tasks seem terribly simple to most people, but at the time, for me, they were the most challenging physical and mental feats of my life. For nearly eight months following my accident, I poured all of my energy into my physical recovery. I wanted to prove wrong everybody who had said that I would never walk again, or that I might always have a severe limp.

Physically, healing was a painful experience. Ten times worse, however, was coping mentally with what seemed to be shattered dreams. The U.S. Department of Defense withdrew my scholarship offers and the Air Force Academy disqualified me for admission based on the results of my physical examination. I was devastated. My father and grandfather had both attended military academies, and I had dreams of becoming a military officer since I was quite young. I was unable to keep my plans to attend the University of Florida for my first collegiate year, and it was impossible for me to do any of the sort of physical activities which for me had always been a means of relieving stress. All of these problems had a pronounced effect on my psychological well being, and I sank into a period of depression. I began to focus less on physical therapy, and life seemed to lose all of it's lustre. This continued for several months, and my mental state got progressively worse.

About a year after the accident, I came to the realization that I was at a point at which I could either give up completely on my recovery and simply choose not to deal with all of the challenges and problems which faced me at that time, or I could find a new direction in life. I clearly remember one morning while I was quietly laying in bed thinking about my future and I realized that I *couldn't* change the past and, if I ever wanted to again to experience the success I enjoyed in life before my I accident, I had better take control of my life, and I needed to do it immediately. It was either sink or swim.

I began by setting a number of goals and carefully outlining the steps I needed to take to accomplish them. I decided that I would ignore the doctors who told me I would never have full use of my leg. I spent an immense amount of time exercising, and I actively participated in all sorts of sports which I had avoided during the previous portion of my recovery. I noticed a sudden improvement in my condition. This provided an immense boost to my self confidence. My doctors were all amazed with my progress. My recovery was so successful, that today, unless my scars are visible, it is essentially impossible to tell that I have had any problems whatsoever with my leg. I proved to myself that anything is possible with hard work.

Now, my future looks brighter than ever . I am living in Washington DC. attending the George Washington University, pursuing a degree in Law. I have submitted a research paper for publication in the *Journal of Geophysical Research*. Additionally, a photograph that I took of lightning was recently published in *National Geographic* magazine. So, you see, I have been to the top of the hill, fallen down, brushed myself off, and climbed straight back up. It can be done. I know I am ultimately much stronger and wiser after my experience. Possibly the most important thing I learned as a result of my accident was that even if circumstances beyond control cause you to lose an opportunity or make a change in your life, If you look hard enough and long enough, you will always find success and happiness in life. I know because I've done it. I now live by the following simple three-rule code which has proven remarkable successful: Don't be afraid to dream, follow your heart, and at all costs, never, never give up.

Sincerely ,

Timothy D. Vislocky

WOODY FRASER
TELEVISION PRODUCER

...is one of the most successful producers of television programming in history. He currently produces two shows for young people on Nickelodeon: "Wild and Crazy Kids" and "What Would You Do?".

Woody Fraser has created, developed, and produced many of television's most successful talk/variety/magazine shows. This list includes one of the most popular and longest running talk shows in history, "The Mike Douglas Show."

Between the years of 1966 and 1973, Woody was responsible for an unprecedented 32 1/2 hours of television programming every week. "The Della Reese Show", "The Bill Russell Show", "The Virginia Graham Show", "The Steve Allen Show", and "Kid Talk" were among that amazing line-up.

Continuing his long record of program innovation, Woody has launched scores of successful programs. Those include "America Alive", "Those Amazing Animals", "People Do The Craziest Things", and "Life's Most Embarrassing Moments" hosted by John Ritter.

Woody Fraser's newest successful show stars Susan Powter as the self-help guru of the '90's in "The Susan Powter Show."

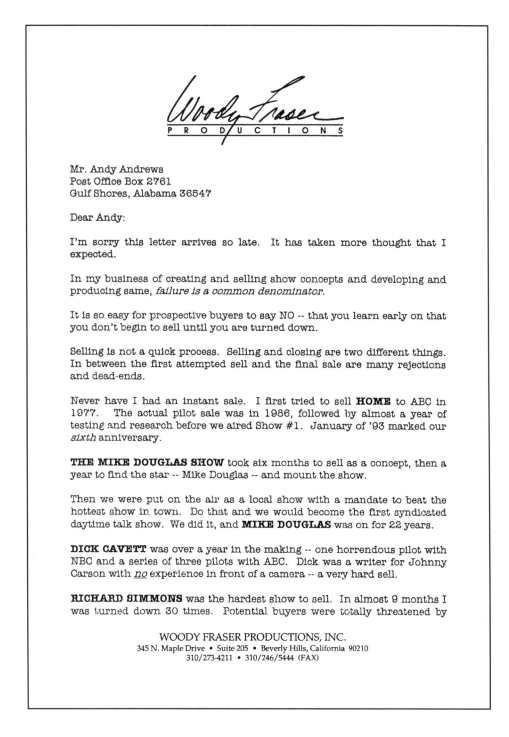

Mr. Andy Andrews
Post Office Box 2761
Gulf Shores, Alabama 36547

Dear Andy:

I'm sorry this letter arrives so late. It has taken more thought that I expected.

In my business of creating and selling show concepts and developing and producing same, *failure is a common denominator.*

It is so easy for prospective buyers to say NO -- that you learn early on that you don't begin to sell until you are turned down.

Selling is not a quick process. Selling and closing are two different things. In between the first attempted sell and the final sale are many rejections and dead-ends.

Never have I had an instant sale. I first tried to sell **HOME** to ABC in 1977. The actual pilot sale was in 1986, followed by almost a year of testing and research before we aired Show #1. January of '93 marked our *sixth* anniversary.

THE MIKE DOUGLAS SHOW took six months to sell as a concept, then a year to find the star -- Mike Douglas -- and mount the show.

Then we were put on the air as a local show with a mandate to beat the hottest show in town. Do that and we would become the first syndicated daytime talk show. We did it, and **MIKE DOUGLAS** was on for 22 years.

DICK CAVETT was over a year in the making -- one horrendous pilot with NBC and a series of three pilots with ABC. Dick was a writer for Johnny Carson with <u>no</u> experience in front of a camera -- a very hard sell.

RICHARD SIMMONS was the hardest show to sell. In almost 9 months I was turned down 30 times. Potential buyers were totally threatened by

WOODY FRASER PRODUCTIONS, INC.
345 N. Maple Drive • Suite 205 • Beverly Hills, California 90210
310/273-4211 • 310/246/5444 (FAX)

Richard's appearance and personality. In the end, I sold a pilot to, of all people, Gene Autry and Golden West Television.

GOOD MORNING AMERICA was different. I was asked to develop the show by Fred Silverman. The difficulties were convincing the network and the audience that we were a bonafide threat to NBC's **TODAY SHOW**. It took four years to push into first place.

THE JIMMY BRESLIN SHOW on ABC late night had the most surprising history. I first wanted to do a show with Breslin in 1976, when he was a short-lived member of my *"one of a kind"* GMA family. *(Jimmy couldn't get up that early.)*

Ten years later in 1986 I sold him to ABC. We did 26 weeks of shows, but Jimmy was very unhappy. The general manager of WABC in New York would not run the show in its prescribed 12:30 a.m. slot. He pushed it to 2:30 a.m. New York is Breslin's world. He was incensed and embarrassed.

At the end of production, I was given a *new* 26 week order. I called Jimmy. His wife told me it was too late, and I should look at this Sunday's Los Angeles Times, New York Times, and Washington Post. Jimmy had taken out an ad -- *firing ABC*. The end of a show and the end of my relationship with Breslin.

Andy, I have a philosophy in my professional life: **NEVER LOOK BACK, AND NEVER TAKE NO FOR AN ANSWER..**

Failure is as inevitable as going to sleep or waking up. It is more important than success. Without the learning process of failure, you will not succeed.

In thinking it over, I have decided to talk about my first failure which led to my first success: **THE MIKE DOUGLAS SHOW**.

What I learned from selling **THE MIKE DOUGLAS SHOW** has molded my approach in developing other shows, such as **GOOD MORNING AMERICA, HOME, THAT'S INCREDIBLE, DICK CAVETT, RICHARD SIMMONS, WILD & CRAZY KIDS**, and others.

Getting **THE MIKE DOUGLAS SHOW** from an idea to a nationally syndicated television program was tough. There were many dead-ends. There were times when I felt like quitting.

WOODY FRASER PRODUCTIONS, INC.
345 N. Maple Drive • Suite 205 • Beverly Hills, California 90210
310/273-4211 • 310/246/5444 (FAX)

I was 22, married with one child and another on the way. As a young TV director in Chicago, I felt that *daytime TV was a desert*. Only game shows, soap operas and giveaway shows glutted the TV schedule on all three networks.

Why not a new show -- one that could entertain, inform and make you laugh. Why not a new type of host -- one who could sing, dance, interview, do comedy, and be a *catalyst*, i.e., make each guest the star instead of himself.
Believe me, there were many *why nots*, as I tried to sell this idea.

I worked for NBC in Chicago at the time. The program manager said *"Don't tell me your idea. You work for me and it will be NBC's idea."*

So naturally -- I *quit*, went back to him and said, *"Here's my great idea!"* And he said, *"Not interested."*

"Why?"

"Your show idea is too expensive to do in daytime. And there is not enough audience to generate the kind of advertising dollars to support this idea of yours."

There I was -- a great idea, and no job.

The other two networks said the same thing to me: *"NO."*

I was frightened. How was I to support this growing family? My "growing" wife *(Baby #2)* told me to keep looking for a way. We would find a way to eat. So, I got mad and began to think.

The key was audience. I was convinced just from the talk among my circle of friends that many more people watched daytime TV than the networks were aware of.

It had to be guilt. People were afraid to admit to rating surveys that they watched daytime television.

So, I pooled my dwindling resources and put three more phone lines into my house. My wife and I and two of our friends took the Chicago phone book and divided it up into 4 areas. We launched our own ratings survey and called over 3,000 people. We would call you on the phone between

WOODY FRASER PRODUCTIONS, INC.
345 N. Maple Drive • Suite 205 • Beverly Hills, California 90210
310/273-4211 • 310/246/5444 (FAX)

10:00 a.m. and 3:00 p.m., saying we were a rating service -- what were you watching? Seven out of ten people said they *weren't watching*.

Then we would say that we were *not* a rating service, but instead were students writing a thesis on **GUILT AND TV**. Immediately, 3 out of those 7 who said they were not watching, changed their minds and told us they *were watching*, but were too embarrassed to admit it.

By my figures, that meant that six out of ten *were* watching -- double what the rating services were getting. I put this together in study form, and began to resell my idea, armed with the new ammunition to answer the *'no audience, no advertising money'* argument.

At the same time, I began to look for a job in non-TV areas and landed a promising interview with an insurance company. The thought of not doing what I really liked scared me even more than running out of money, so I re-doubled my efforts to sell my idea.

The networks had laughed at me. But, Don McGannon, president of Group W - Westinghouse TV did not. He bought the concept and the study idea, and sent me to Cleveland to develop what eventually became **THE MIKE DOUGLAS SHOW**.

The show lasted 22 years. In that time, I have created and produced many other shows. I have also produced 8 children. I have tried to teach them to be passionate about their interests and follow them enthusiastically and doggedly. They all share my enthusiasm for life. They also use failure as a learning ground -- one incident to be applied to new ventures leading to success.

I wonder if I had not pursued my first dream -- an idea that no one seemed to want -- how it would have affected the way I raise and counsel my kids?

Thanks, Andy. Good luck with this book -- it's a good idea. Don't let anyone tell you differently.

Sincerely,

Woody Fraser

WOODY FRASER PRODUCTIONS, INC.
345 N. Maple Drive • Suite 205 • Beverly Hills, California 90210
310/273-4211 • 310/246/5444 (FAX)

"I find the great thing
in this world is,
not so much where we stand,
as in what direction
we are moving."

Goethe

GARY SMALLEY
AUTHOR/SPEAKER

...is President of "Today's Family" in Branson, Missouri. He is the author of twelve best-selling books.

Gary Smalley has spent years learning, teaching, and counseling others with a unique, energetic and encouraging approach. He has personally interviewed hundreds of singles and couples; surveying thousands of people at his seminars. He asks two critical questions: "What is it that strengthens our relationships and what weakens them?"

As a family expert, it should be noted that Gary's greatest asset is his own family. He and his wife Norma have had a close-knit marriage for 29 years. During that time they have raised three children, all of whom have become extremely successful in their chosen fields.

Gary's career has given him broad exposure in many different markets. A frequent guest on such programs as "Oprah Winfrey" and "Focus on the Family", he has done hundreds of radio and television interviews over the past twenty years.

Gary's commitment to helping others build strong relationships places him in an unusual position. He is one of the leading family experts in the world today—and he is accepted by those in all walks of life.

HCR 4 - 2211 LakeShore Dr.
Branson, Missouri 65616
(417) 335-4321
FAX (417) 336-3515

Dear Andy,

Thank you for your book, "Storms of Perfection". As I read through the pages, I was deeply encouraged to see all the good and exciting things that can come out of perceived failure. It made me feel like I was part of a special "fraternity" for the wounded.

I've spent my entire life swimming through the same types of storms you illustrated in your book. I was your typical impressionable child who believed what people said about me and agreed that I was doomed to be "average". How could I ever be anything more. My mother had only gone through the eighth grade in school, so, it makes more sense to me today why she and my teacher talked me into repeating the third grade. They told me I'd be a "leader" next year. As it turned out, no one ever really encouraged me to excel in school. I took my first book home to study in my senior year of high school. None of my four brothers or sisters went to college. I believed that only a few "natural students" got in. Where do kids ever pick up these ideas?

But despite all the "failure" thoughts ringing in my head, I had a deep feeling that somehow something good was going to happen some day. But when these positive thoughts came, the negative thinking usually smothered them.

Then finally, a real life changing, positive thinking, hopeful, and dream filled attitude came to me in the middle of what could have easily been my most defeating experience. At the time, I had been working over ten years for one of America's most successful marriage enriching seminar organizations. Without warning, I was pushed out of this organization. Consequently, I was very depressed, feeling like my life was over. Without the organization, I didn't see how I could ever again do what I loved most - assist others with their marriages and families. I was at the lowest point of my life; I couldn't eat for several days; and then I discovered the most calming, positive and hopeful words I've ever read. They since have been my strength through many setbacks and failures and have allowed me to live each day with great anticipation.

These simple yet profound statements have given me patience to wait on the good things in life because I now know "it's just a matter of time before my dreams come true". The first powerful truth I learned was, "When you're in trouble, cry out to God and He **will** rescue you." That truth was all I had for months. The second was, "Seek and you will find, ask and it will be given to you, knock and the door **will** be opened up to you." I follow this counsel everyday, and I've yet to see an unanswered request. The final truth I learned was, "God **will** provide much more for His children than they ask for, but only to those who ask Him persistently." I can attest that the more persistent I have been, the more rewards God blesses me with.

When I was at the bottom, in childlike faith, I simply reached out to Him. For the past twenty years, I've watched His hand in fulfilling all of my dreams. Some have taken 20 years to come true and others didn't come about the way I thought they would. Still, my dreams have come about by waiting for Him to open the door or provide the opportunity. Someone once gave me a great statement which taught me I have to prepare for His opportunities: "If you ask God for a horse, you'd better start learning how to ride."

It's been exciting to have sold over four million books to help families, and to have had over twenty million people around the world watch a portion of our marriage videos. Just yesterday we heard that our T. V. half hour infommercial won the top national award for this year. I can honestly say that all of this came as a result of my previous failures.

Setbacks and failures are no match to clearly defined dreams, persistent seeking of those same dreams, and watching the might of a faithful God.

Your admirer for life,

Gary Smalley
President Today's Family

GS:tln

ELIZABETH TAYLOR
ACTRESS

...is an Academy Award winner. She started her career at the age of nine and has now starred in the films of six different decades.

No other international personality has sparked the intense public fascination that Elizabeth Taylor has engendered throughout her unparalleled career.

As an Academy Award winning actress, Elizabeth Taylor has captured hearts and minds around the world with a life and career that have labeled her a survivor and a pioneer in all her very public endeavors. The subject of countless profiles and much speculation, Elizabeth Taylor remains a woman of strength despite fierce public scrutiny.

Elizabeth Taylor is no stranger to life's trials and tribulations, but she has chosen to learn from these experiences and make use of their lessons. Her success as a performer and a businesswoman have given her the time and platform to support numerous philanthropic projects around the world.

ELIZABETH TAYLOR

Andy Andrews
P.O. Box 2761
Gulf Shores, AL 36547

Dear Andy,

Your letter to me was most interesting because it is so true that people think I have always had things go my way. Indeed, I have been very fortunate in my acting career to garner choice roles and to have the opportunity to star with so many wonderful people. Of course, my personal life, which I do not wish to talk about here, has certainly had its ups and downs. Suffice it to say that I have learned, through the grace of God, to roll with the punches and not worry about what other people think. I am, above all, a survivor.

What nearly did undo me was when I approached the Hollywood community in 1985 for my first AIDS benefit. I must say I was totally unprepared for the unqualified rejection I received on all fronts. Everyone said I was just on another one of my crusades and they blew me off!

At first I felt a tremendous sense of rejection -- then I was infuriated. The incredibly homophobic attitude of my peers toward homosexuals and AIDS was just so unfair. Certainly Hollywood would never have become what it is today without the marvelous creativity of homosexuals, yet most of my contemporaries were turning their backs on their own! And in doing so, they were also turning their backs on me! That was a new and not very happy experience.

But I got over it. I decided that I had no right to be angry if I wasn't prepared to fight for what I believed in. So I turned that rejection and anger around and I chose to use my celebrity to fight even harder. As I did that, people slowly began to come around.

It's been a long, hard fight -- and, tragically, we still don't have a cure for AIDS. But Hollywood has rallied, and some of those peers who rejected me and my fight against AIDS have become some of my staunchest supporters. It just goes to show that when you keep your goals uppermost in your mind, and don't let the rejection deter you, anything is possible. It's that thought that keeps me going, because I will never stop until that cure if found.

Sincerely,

Elizabeth Taylor

CLEBE McCLARY
VIETNAM VETERAN / AUTHOR / SPEAKER

...is the recipient of three Purple Hearts. The President of the United States personally presented him with the Bronze Star and Silver Star. His life story is told in the autobiography "Living Proof".

Clebe McClary is an American hero. He is also a personal hero of mine. I met Clebe for the first time when I was twelve years old. He had spoken at our church the night before and that afternoon beat my Dad in a round of golf...with one hand. My father was amazed and our family never forgot him.

Almost twenty years later, we were reacquainted by our mutual friends, Bubba and Sandy Pratt. Clebe and his wife, Deanna, have now become personal heros to thousands of people. Together, they are among the most sought after speakers in America.

A little known fact about Clebe is that he holds the record for the Balke treadmill stress test at the renowned Cooper Clinic in Dallas, Texas. This is the same record shot at and missed by every member of the Dallas Cowboys! Clebe McClary is "Living Proof" that with the right attitude...all things are possible.

CLEBE McCLARY

P.O. Box 535 • Pawleys Island, SC 29585 • (803) 237-2582 • FAX (803) 237-1890

Andy Andrews
P. O. Box 2761
Gulf Shores, AL 36547

Dear Andy,

Thank you very much for considering us to be in your book, STORMS OF PERFECTION. We have weathered a few storms. In fact, I spent 2 1/2 years in the hospital and 34 major operations, after being wounded seven times in Vietnam.

Deanna, my wife, wrote a book, COMMITMENT TO LOVE. Her genuine love was a significant part of my recovery, and I wouldn't be here without my wonderful wife. I'm certain God had a purpose and a plan for my life, but she's the one who gave me a reason and a "want to" to live the night I was blown to pieces on a hill in Vietnam.

My nineteenth and last patrol was a tough one. March 3, 1968, my wife's birthday, was not a celebration night for me. My team was under enemy siege, and I knew it was going to be a long night. I had two men killed and eight seriously wounded. I have never wanted to live so badly. I wanted to see my men get off that hill alive and then to see my wife one more time.

One special Marine, Ralph Johnson, saved my life by covering a grenade with his body. Ralph is another reason I am challenged to help others appreciate how precious life is. One of my Marines, who had two brothers killed in Vietnam, had this inscription on his lighter: "You have never lived, until you've nearly died." That really means something to me!

I remember very well the day Deanna walked into the room to see me at Bethesda Naval Hospital. She didn't even recognize me and turned to walk out. I called to her, "Hey, Honey, it's me. I know I'm not too pretty to look at, but I thank God I'm alive to be with you today." I was aware that there were many wives who kept on walking and who never looked back, but Deanna has stood by me for 26 years. I truly thank God for her.

I can say from experience the storms we've had in our lives have made us a stronger couple. We have fortified the bunker! Our home, love and marriage have been strengthened during the weak times, because we chose to exercise our grit, determination and steadfast faithfulness in order to grow.

We realize that changes come in everyone's life. Mine were visibly physical, with the loss of an arm and an eye. I hope most people won't have to endure a battlefield experience and maybe they'll never experience a crippling disease or a tragic accident, but they <u>have</u> been laid off from work, struggled with financial problems or some other problems that have caused them to face major changes. We found that Romans 5:3-5 has served as a source of encouragement to us. "We rejoice in our suffering, because suffering produces endurance, endurance produces character, character produces hope and hope doesn't disappoint us, because God's love has been poured into our hearts as a free gift from the Holy Spirit." <u>His</u> strength, principles and hope have challenged us to press on regardless of circumstances!

Several acronyms I use to weather the storms in life are:
PATCH, because I wear one on my eye. It reminds me that it is a <u>P</u>ositive <u>A</u>ttitude <u>T</u>hat <u>C</u>reates <u>H</u>ope. I don't mean an attitude that comes and goes from some video or motivational talk, but a positive attitude that is developed from Bible study, Scripture memorization and prayer - the truth that sets man free.
BIONIC: <u>B</u>elieve <u>I</u>t or <u>N</u>ot, <u>I</u> <u>C</u>are. Andy, I care about you and your family, and I think we need to care about others. Husbands need to care about their wives, wives need to care about their husbands, and let them know that they care.
FIDO has become my motto. It's the license tag on my car. <u>F</u>orget <u>I</u>t and <u>D</u>rive <u>O</u>n. I'm not talking about forgetting people - they're precious. Just forget about your problems; don't dwell on them. Good experience, bad experience, learn from it and get on with your life.

As a Marine, FIDO and Semper Fidelis mean always faithful. Men and women, we need to be faithful to our spouses, our families, and our Country. Two of the biggest problems in America today are Aids and abortion. We could cure both of these by being faithful. If we were faithful, we wouldn't even have these problems!

I appreciate what you're doing, Andy. Keep on caring and giving of yourself. Let me know if we can ever help you in any way. It's been an honor to be part of your life's work. I guarantee you, you've been a tremendous part of ours. The <u>rest</u> of your life will be the <u>best</u> of your life because you are investing in the lives of others!

In His Grip,

Clebe & Deanna McClary
P. O. Box 535
Pawleys Island, SC 29585   (803) 237-2582   FAX (803) 237-1890

"Have I not commanded you?
Be strong and courageous!
Do not tremble or be dismayed,
for the Lord your God is with you
wherever you go."

Joshua 1:9

CHARLIE CHASE
TELEVISION PERSONALITY

...is the co-host of "Music City Tonight" on TNN. With Lorianne Crook, he also hosts "The Nashville Record Review," a four hour radio program heard on more than 300 stations in the United States, Japan, and the United Kingdom.

When I am around Charlie Chase, chances are I will be laughing. Charlie has that gift. He will make you laugh. That has been a big part of his success. He is also unpredictable. That facet of his personality has led to a series of highly popular television specials titled "Funny Business" in which he plays practical jokes on unsuspecting country music stars.

As talk show hosts, Charlie and his partner, Lorianne Crook, are without peer. Their questions are sharp and interesting and their focus always seems to be on making the guest look good. The genuine chemistry between the two and their obvious talent is the major reason that "Music City Tonight" is one of the best shows on television.

Charlie started his career at the age of thirteen so he has spent most of his life in front of a microphone or camera. If you are fortunate enough to meet him in person, you will see that he is also a great guy in "real life"!

Dear Andy,

Thanks for the invitation to share some thoughts in your new book. I really enjoyed the first one.

In all the years I've interviewed and personally visited with the top names in business and entertainment, I've found that they have always set goals and kept focusing on them until they reached them. Their time frames were from a few years, to as many as 15 or 20, and some, deemed successful by many, felt they had not reached their potential yet. The bottom line was, they were always reaching for that immediately unattainable goal.

Then it hit me, I've often reflected on this, and my philosophy has been totally different. It may have something to do with the fact I found something career wise, early in life, that I really enjoyed. I have loved broadcasting since I first started at age 13 in Rogersville, Tennessee. Looking back on my career, I found that I didn't look at a certain goal and focus on it. Instead, I always concentrated on and enjoyed what I was doing in the present and found that hard work brought the goals and opportunities to me.

For me personally, I guess it boils down to this...Don't focus on the future. Concentrate and do your best with your present opportunities. If you're not careful, you may find yourself going in the wrong direction, thinking too much about the future and neglecting what you're doing now.

A final note - Don't let your career run your life. Let your life run your career.

Best regards,

Charlie Chase

Jim Owens & Associates, Inc.
1525 McGavock Street • Nashville, TN 37203-3131
615/256-7700 • Fax 615/256-7779

155

J. B. HUNT
ENTREPRENEUR

...is an active chairman overseeing J.B. Hunt Transportation Services, Inc. He was most recently named to the Board of Directors of the Texas Mexican Railroad.

The explosive growth of J.B. Hunt Transportation can only be attributed to the man himself—J.B. Hunt. His imagination, determination to succeed, and ability to overcome obstacles are reasons why he owns the largest truckload carrier in the United States.

J.B. Hunt now employs over 11,000 people who utilize his 7,000 trucks and 17,000 trailers. This is quite an accomplishment for one with such humble roots, but as you will see in his letter, the years of sacrifice, exhaustion, and dejection were all a part of building a successful empire.

In his sixties, J.B. Hunt remains dedicated to a number of other organizations as well. He is currently a member of the board of Daystar, Inc., a media ministry of the First Baptist Church of Springdale. He is also a member of the Arkansas Business Council and the Director of the American Trucking Association Foundation. In May 1991, Mr. Hunt was honored by the Arkansas Motor Carriers Association as the first inductee in the AMCA Hall of Fame.

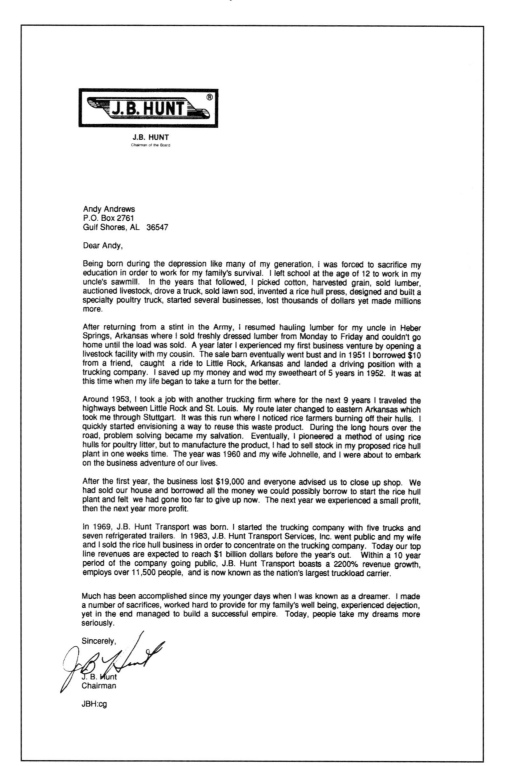

J.B. HUNT
Chairman of the Board

Andy Andrews
P.O. Box 2761
Gulf Shores, AL 36547

Dear Andy,

Being born during the depression like many of my generation, I was forced to sacrifice my education in order to work for my family's survival. I left school at the age of 12 to work in my uncle's sawmill. In the years that followed, I picked cotton, harvested grain, sold lumber, auctioned livestock, drove a truck, sold lawn sod, invented a rice hull press, designed and built a specialty poultry truck, started several businesses, lost thousands of dollars yet made millions more.

After returning from a stint in the Army, I resumed hauling lumber for my uncle in Heber Springs, Arkansas where I sold freshly dressed lumber from Monday to Friday and couldn't go home until the load was sold. A year later I experienced my first business venture by opening a livestock facility with my cousin. The sale barn eventually went bust and in 1951 I borrowed $10 from a friend, caught a ride to Little Rock, Arkansas and landed a driving position with a trucking company. I saved up my money and wed my sweetheart of 5 years in 1952. It was at this time when my life began to take a turn for the better.

Around 1953, I took a job with another trucking firm where for the next 9 years I traveled the highways between Little Rock and St. Louis. My route later changed to eastern Arkansas which took me through Stuttgart. It was this run where I noticed rice farmers burning off their hulls. I quickly started envisioning a way to reuse this waste product. During the long hours over the road, problem solving became my salvation. Eventually, I pioneered a method of using rice hulls for poultry litter, but to manufacture the product, I had to sell stock in my proposed rice hull plant in one weeks time. The year was 1960 and my wife Johnelle, and I were about to embark on the business adventure of our lives.

After the first year, the business lost $19,000 and everyone advised us to close up shop. We had sold our house and borrowed all the money we could possibly borrow to start the rice hull plant and felt we had gone too far to give up now. The next year we experienced a small profit, then the next year more profit.

In 1969, J.B. Hunt Transport was born. I started the trucking company with five trucks and seven refrigerated trailers. In 1983, J.B. Hunt Transport Services, Inc. went public and my wife and I sold the rice hull business in order to concentrate on the trucking company. Today our top line revenues are expected to reach $1 billion dollars before the year's out. Within a 10 year period of the company going public, J.B. Hunt Transport boasts a 2200% revenue growth, employs over 11,500 people, and is now known as the nation's largest truckload carrier.

Much has been accomplished since my younger days when I was known as a dreamer. I made a number of sacrifices, worked hard to provide for my family's well being, experienced dejection, yet in the end managed to build a successful empire. Today, people take my dreams more seriously.

Sincerely,

J. B. Hunt
Chairman

JBH:cg

ROGER STAUBACH
FORMER NFL QUARTERBACK

…was elected to the Pro Football Hall of Fame in 1985, his first year of eligibility.

Few players at any level of football ever generated as much excitement as Roger Staubach every time he took a snap from center. If one characteristic symbolized his daring play more than any other, it was the ability to lead the Dallas Cowboys to come-from-behind victories. He engineered no less than 23 fourth quarter comebacks that produced victories—14 in the final two minutes of the game! Roger led the Cowboys to four Super Bowls and achieved victories in Super Bowls VI and XII.

Roger received a late start in professional football as he fulfilled four years active duty with the United States Navy after graduating from the Naval Academy. He separated from active duty as a lieutenant following a distinguished career that included overseas duty in Vietnam.

Roger left a legacy at Annapolis. As a junior in 1963, he was named the recipient of college football's highest honor, the Heisman Trophy. He was also the only midshipman to win the Thompson Trophy Cup for best all around athlete three consecutive years.

Roger Staubach has carried over the same winning attitude and traits from his successful football career into his business career. Today, he is Chairman of the Board and Chief Executive Officer of The Staubach Company, an integrated real estate company that provides services related to office, industrial, and retail.

PERSONALITIES
INTERNATIONAL

Mr. Andy Andrews
P.O. Box 1732
Nashville, Tennessee 37217

Dear Andy:

It was preseason, 1972. After serving in the Navy for four years and suffering three long years as second string quarterback for the Dallas Cowboys, I had finally won the starting position and we were coming off our first Super Bowl win.

The Super Bowl team was pretty much in tact, so we walked into training camp feeling good. We were in the Coliseum for our annual preseason game against the Rams. I felt I could make some extra yards running the ball on a play, but Marlin McKeever had other ideas. As a result of an error in judgement on that play, I had to have surgery on my shoulder and was out for the season.

That was an extremely difficult time for me. Not only was it physically painful to rehabilitate the arm, but it was mentally difficult to once again be on the bench as an observer. Also, having had a late start in pro football, I felt the clock was ticking and I would have to again compete for the starting position.

I did persevere and as soon as I was physically able, I was working out, attending meetings and practices, and studying the game plan as though I would be playing on Sunday. The team made it to the playoffs and although I didn't start in the San Francisco game, I did finish it. We were able to come from behind and score two touchdowns in the last 1 1/2 minutes to win the game.

Fortunately, I learned early in life that if you work hard and are prepared, when you are called on to perform you will be able to accomplish your goals. It takes a lot of unspectacular preparation to achieve spectacular results.

Sincerely,

Roger Staubach
Partner

MARY KAY ASH
ENTREPRENEUR

....is the founder of Mary Kay Cosmetics. The company now has 325,000 independent Beauty Consultants in 21 countries worldwide.

One has only to see a soft pink Cadillac to know that the name "Mary Kay" will be in the back window. This is just one of the rewards that Mary Kay Ash uses to motivate and encourage her beauty consultants to have a successful business.

Mary Kay's dreams and willingness to go out on a limb when everyone and everything said she shouldn't are what have made her one of the wealthiest women in the cosmetics industry today.

In 1994, Mary Kay Cosmetics was included for the second time on the Fortune 500 list of the largest industrial companies in America. It was listed for the second time among "The 100 Best Companies to Work for in America", in 1993, and among "The 10 Best for Women." Mary Kay Cosmetics has enjoyed eight consecutive years of record sales.

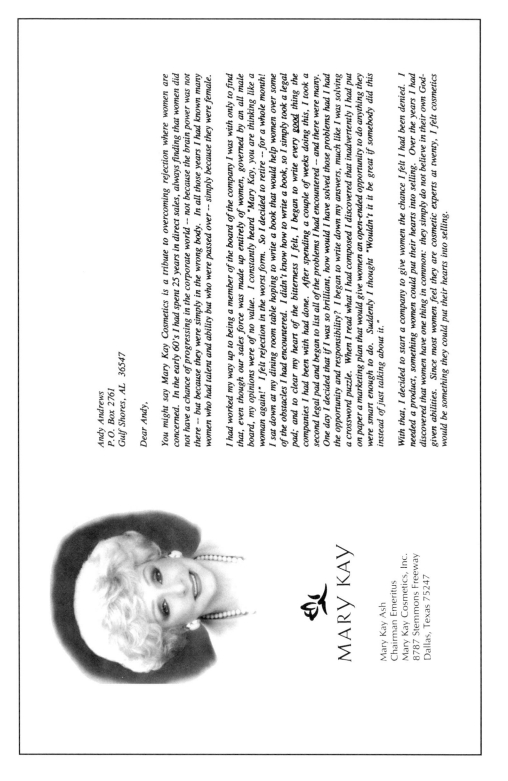

MARY KAY

Mary Kay Ash
Chairman Emeritus
Mary Kay Cosmetics, Inc.
8787 Stemmons Freeway
Dallas, Texas 75247

Andy Andrews
P.O. Box 2761
Gulf Shores, AL   36547

Dear Andy,

You might say Mary Kay Cosmetics is a tribute to overcoming rejection where women are concerned. In the early 60's I had spent 25 years in direct sales, always finding that women did not have a chance of progressing in the corporate world -- not because the brain power was not there -- but because they were simply in the wrong body. In all those years I had known many women who had talent and ability but who were passed over -- simply because they were female.

I had worked my way up to being a member of the board of the company I was with only to find that, even though our sales force was made up entirely of women, governed by an all male board, my opinions were of no value. I constantly heard "Mary Kay, you are thinking like a woman again!" I felt rejection in the worst form. So I decided to retire -- for a whole month! I sat down at my dining room table hoping to write a book that would help women over some of the obstacles I had encountered. I didn't know how to write a book, so I simply took a legal pad; and to clear my heart of the bitterness I felt, I began to write every good thing the companies I had been with had done. After spending a couple of weeks doing this, I took a second legal pad and began to list all of the problems I had encountered -- and there were many. One day I decided that if I was so brilliant, how would I have solved those problems had I had the opportunity and responsibility? I began to write down my answers, much like I was solving a crossword puzzle. When I read what I had composed I discovered that inadvertently I had put on paper a marketing plan that would give women an open-ended opportunity to do anything they were smart enough to do. Suddenly I thought "Wouldn't it it be great if somebody did this instead of just talking about it."

With that, I decided to start a company to give women the chance I felt I had been denied. I needed a product, something women could put their hearts into selling. Over the years I had discovered that women have one thing in common: they simply do not believe in their own God-given abilities. Since most women feel they are cosmetic experts at twenty, I felt cosmetics would be something they could put their hearts into selling.

Page 2
Andy Andrews

Ten years before, in 1953, I had met a woman who had developed a cosmetic that I felt was the best one I had every used. She had died in 1961, never having gotten her product on the market to any extent. She had tried to sell it out of a little home beauty shop in the wrong end of town. As we say in Texas, "That dog won't hunt!" I was able to purchase the formulations from her heirs. Now I had a marketing plan and a product.

I went to my attorney to set up my little corporation. His answer was, "Mary Kay, if you are going to throw away your life savings, why don't you just go directly to the trash can. It will be so much easier than what you are proposing." To further "encourage" me he sent to Washington for a pamphlet telling me how many cosmetic companies went broke <u>every day</u>!

My accountant agreed with him, telling me I would go broke in six weeks, that I couldn't pay the commissions I was proposing. Further, I would never get a loan to enhance my $5,000 savings (a woman applying for a loan to start a business in those days would have been laughed right out the door). I responded, "I think people will support that which they help to create." I left more determined than ever to proceed with my "great idea."

To add to this rejection, since I knew nothing about administration, I assigned that task to my husband who had expertise in that area. When he tried to talk to me about the percentages, I must admit I didn't listen! In my mind that was his problem. I was working on the "important" things, the product, the jars, a training manual, and recruiting our first Beauty Consultants. One month to the day before we were to open our doors, when every single penny I had was spent or committed, my husband died of a heart attack at the breakfast table! I suddenly realized I had only half a company and that I would have to go back to work immediately for someone else if I did not go on with "my" company.

162

Page 3
Andy Andrews

I had always believed that "when God closes a door, He always opens a window." That window came in the form of my 20-year-old son. The day of my husband's funeral my two sons and my daughter and I sat down to decide what I should do. Richard, the youngest of the three children, said, "Mother, I will move to Dallas tomorrow to help you." How would you like to turn your life savings over to your 20 year old? I must say that if Richard had a brain, I didn't know about it. Little did I know that just five years later he would be awarded the American Marketing Association's "Man of the Year" award and today is recognized as one of America's young financial geniuses!! My daughter, Marylyn, offered to take the first showcase to Houston and start there. My older son, Ben, offered his help, too, and six years later became part of the Company.

That was the inauspicious start of Mary Kay Cosmetics on Friday, September 13, 1963 (nobody starts a company on the 13th -- but we did!). In 1991 (again on Friday 13th of December) we hit the BILLION DOLLAR mark in retail sales!! We now have more than 250,000 Beauty Consultants worldwide, and we are presently in 18 countries around the world.

Sincerely,

Mary Kay

Mary Kay
Chairman Emeritus

MKA:tr

BEN
PETERS
SONGWRITER

...started playing and singing at the age of fourteen. He has since won countless Grammy Awards and was named "Songwriter of the Year" in 1975.

Ben's home in Nashville is beautiful. But the most impressive thing to me was the gold and platinum albums...everywhere. I have never seen anything like it in my life. The awards were literally stacked in closets and corners.

Ben Peter's music is known around the world. It is impossible to pass a jukebox that doesn't contain one of his songs. "Kiss An Angel Good Morning" and "Before the Next Teardrop Falls" are just two of the hits that landed Ben in the Nashville Songwriter's Association International Hall of Fame.

Ben also knows about persistence and it has paid off. His songs have sold over 100 million copies.

B   E   N   P   E   T   E   R   S   M   U   S   I   C

Andy Andrews
P.O. Box 2761
Gulf Shores, Alabama 36547

Dear Andy,

I started playing in bands when I was 14 years old. I quit after I got my wings in the navy and married my wife, Jackie. Still wanting to be involved in music, I started fooling around with writing. We moved to Jackson, Mississippi, where I took a job at a record company but nothing developed there so we went to Atlanta for two years, writing part time while working at an insurance company.

I wrote a few songs and we made a few trips to Nashville but we kept getting the songs rejected. I was ready to give up. I told Jackie, "If we don't hear something encouraging today, I'm gonna quit trying and move on up in the insurance industry." I got in the car and went for a drive to think things out and when I got back home Jackie was waiting out front for me. Nashville had called and liked one of my songs, and wanted to sign me as a writer. We went up and signed but still had nothing recorded.

Shortly thereafter, the company signed me as professional manager and we moved to Music City. My job was to pitch the songs in the catalogue and get them recorded. The problem was, the songs had already been turned down time after time before I got there. Every time I pitched I got rejected.

All this was extremely frustrating to say the least. I soon realized that if I was going to get anything recorded I was going to have to write it. I didn't know anything about country music. We put the radio on a country station 24 hours a day and went backstage at the old Opry house every Friday and Saturday night to learn about the people and the music.

In the middle of all this, Broadcast Music, Inc., who collects performance royalties from radio, TV, etc. for the writers and publishers, wrote me a letter suggesting I end my agreement with them due to lack of activity. I wrote them back to please hang in there with me a little while longer. I busted my brain, burned some midnight oil and I guess I started zeroing in.

After about 4 months we had a top 5 record on "If The Whole World Stopped Lovin'," followed by a number one hit by Eddy Arnold called "Turn The World Around." Fortunately these were followed by quite a few more.

All that rejection almost got me, but I'm sure glad I didn't fold. The song they liked in Nashville when they called, has never been recorded. My four year contract as manager expired and I started my own company and the years since have been good to us.

Andy, thanks for asking. Hope to see you on the Island soon.

Your Friend,

Ben Peters

HARRY BLACKSTONE, JR.
MAGICIAN

...holds the record for the largest and longest running illusion and magic show in the history of New York theater.

Every time Harry Blackstone steps on stage for a performance, he brings with him the legacy of an American theatrical tradition that dates back over a century. Harry is the gifted son and professional heir of The Great Blackstone, America's legendary magical genius who led the art of illusion to heights never achieved before his era.

The son is doing a great deal more than merely following in his father's footsteps. Harry Blackstone is an author, an actor, an inventor, a casino showroom headliner, a television personality, a teacher, and the creator and performer of the longest running magic and illusion show ever to play Broadway.

No magician in history has been more honored by his peers than Harry Blackstone. Named "Magician of the Year" in 1979 and 1985 by the Academy of Magical Arts, Harry is currently the Society of American Magician's "International Ambassador of Magic". He is also a recipient of the coveted "Star of Magic" which is an honor bestowed to only eleven other magicians in history, including his father.

From whatever magical place The Great Blackstone is looking down on his son's dazzling success—it's a sure bet that he is smiling and very proud.

BLACKSTONE MAGIK ENTERPRISES, INC.

Andy Andrews
P.O. Box 2761
Gulf Shores, AL 36547

Dear Andy,

You know, when I was growing up, it seems all of other kids I associated with looked up to their parents. I was no exception. I looked up to my Dad and I wanted to be like him. But, I came to realize fairly early that I lived with two fathers – one a gentle, loving man with an outrageous sense of humor and a giving, sharing personality and the other -- a living legend, known by the world as "The Great Blackstone."

When your father or your mother is famous in their profession, whether it be as a doctor, a lawyer, or an entertainer, the general public views them as bigger than life. And as much as I wanted to be like my Dad , as I grew to be a teenager and gave thought to what I would do with my life, I didn't want to compete with the legend for fear of not making him proud.

My father had very little formal education (he only finished the 8th grade!). He put great stock in education and had a great love of knowledge. Dad collected quotes, which he shared frequently. He always stressed a good education to me and the importance he placed upon it seems best expressed in one of his favorite quotes: "Whatever is between your ears can't be taken away!"

Because of Dad's desire for me to have that good education, and because theatres were not air conditioned during the earlier part of the century, I was in various boarding schools around the country from the age of five, while Dad was "on the road" every year performing from Labor Day to Memorial Day. He performed professionally from 1899 to 1964, just before he died in 1965. Dad was 50 years old when I was born and our relationship was that of father, grandfather and friend.

The rest of my family consisted of the people who traveled with his show. And it was an entourage of characters. My dad's brother, Uncle Pete, and his wife, Millie, as well as the on-stage assistants who were only a few years older than I. Uncle Pete and Aunt Millie, the cast and the crew were like self-appointed big brothers uncles, aunts and sisters with many of the same conflicts and joys of a big family, but nevertheless a real family.

I took my father's advice and studied hard. After attending Swarthmore College in Pennsylvania, I did my duty to our great country and continued my education in the Army Language School, and was then sent on an all expense paid trip to Korea. I also was graduated from the University of Southern California and earned a Master's Degree from the University of Texas.

After acquiring all this education and life experience, I was faced with a decision about what do to as a profession. Well, as you might guess, I wanted to be in the entertainment field, so I went into radio and television broadcasting. It was a similar profession and I was in the entertainment field, but I couldn't be compared directly to Dad. I then worked in political campaigns with the family of the radio/TV station I worked for in Austin, Texas for Lyndon Johnson, and later I tried my hand in the corporate world with Tupperware, but entertainment was still my desire. When the opportunity came along to work in television production with The Smothers Brothers, Glenn Campbell and Sonny and Cher, I grabbed it.

But, something was still missing. I wasn't looking just for a job, I wanted to find the profession that would become an avocation. No matter who or what I was working for, I found myself spending weekends and vacations doing magic shows around the country, but I never considered these performances my "real job."

Then, fortuitously, due to a series of events at CBS, all of us at "The Smothers Brothers Comedy Hour" were out of work. Not knowing what to do, I fell back on my week-end/vacation hobby and to my great surprise, Magic was my calling. Friends of my father were supportive and I had never been happier. I discovered I had no reason to feel intimidated or unworthy when it game to my father and his reputation. I was my own person with my own style of performance, which has grown, developed and matured with each performance.

Each and every time I step on stage, the joy, excitement and pure love of what I'm doing engulfs me. The fact that what I do gives great joy to people, that not only do I entertain, but for the time I'm on stage I can ease someone's load and make them laugh or smile or be amazed by an illusion, motivates me more than I ever thought possible.

Today, after more years as a professional magician than I care to admit, I'm delighted the "legend" I grew up with no longer holds me in awe, but instead fills me with gratitude. Doors were opened due to my father, but they would close even faster if I wasn't able to hold my own. I know how lucky and blessed I am because I love what I do.

Sincerely,

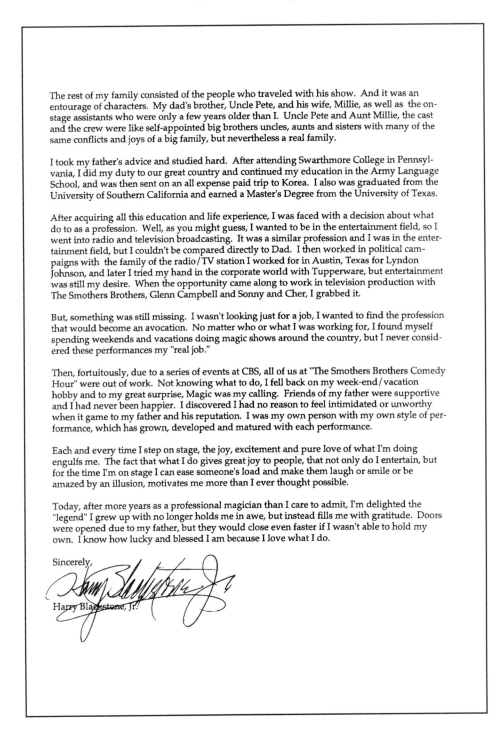

Harry Blackstone, Jr.

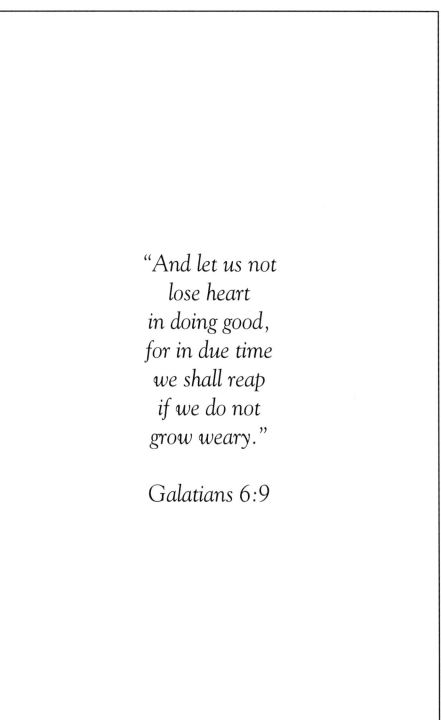

"And let us not
lose heart
in doing good,
for in due time
we shall reap
if we do not
grow weary."

Galatians 6:9

BOONE PICKENS
ENTREPRENEUR

…is the Chairman and Chief Executive Officer of MESA and Chairman of the Natural Gas Vehicle Coalition.

It seems only natural that a boy growing up in an oil town in eastern Oklahoma would seek his destiny in the same field as his father. Boone attributes much of his success to his mother and father. "My parents taught me early that hard work, honesty, and ambition are the keys to success." He has since expanded on that philosophy. When asked how to succeed, he states, "Come early. Stay late. Work hard. Play by the rules. Never cheat to win. Stay physically fit. I promise you, you'll beat the competition and you'll have fun doing it."

Some 40 years ago, Boone Pickens turned a $2,500 investment into one of the nation's largest independent natural gas and oil producers. During that time, he has become known as a pioneer advocate for shareholders rights, founding the United Shareholders Association in 1986.

Boone's career has been marked by a commitment to higher education. Over the last ten years he has spoken to over 100,000 students on college campuses. It's no wonder that his autobiography was on the New York Times Best Seller List.

As you will see in Mr. Pickens letter, becoming successful is no deterrent to challenges in one's life. The proper attitude and experience, however, do put it all in perspective.

Boone Pickens
chairman of the board & chief executive officer

MESA

Mr. Andy Andrews
P. O. Box 2761
Gulf Shores AL 36542

Dear Andy:

Unfortunately, I've had my share of setbacks in life, and I don't like to think back on them. Instead, I prefer focusing on the opportunities ahead. But, since you asked...

My biggest setback came in 1985. That was when I predicted natural gas prices would begin increasing. MESA is one of the nation's largest natural gas producers and, based on that projection, we began acquiring new reserves and increasing our shareholder dividends. In fact, between 1986 and 1990, MESA bought over $1.7 billion of properties and distributed $1.1 billion to our shareholders.

Unfortunately, the gas price dropped by 50 percent over a five-year period. In retrospect, if we hadn't distributed so much money to our shareholders, we wouldn't have been stuck with so much debt -- $1.2 billion in all -- going into the 1990s. It goes without saying that MESA's shareholders took a beating. Since I am a MESA shareholder, I took a bath, too. Because I missed on the gas price and MESA's stock price went down, my net worth fell by more than $100 million.

Needless to say, it's not my fondest memory of the 1980s.

Sincerely,

Boone Pickens

jr

ALPHABETICAL INDEX

For booking information,

additional copies of this book or Volume I,

available in both English and Spanish;

or to see other popular items by Andy Andrews

such as comedy cassettes, motivational tapes

and a variety of t-shirts, please call for a free color brochure.

1-800-726-ANDY

24 hours a day

or you may write to:

Andy Andrews

P.O. Box 17321

Nashville, TN 37217

USA